GENIUS MOM HACKS

Genius Mom Hacks

The Tools and Routines That Will Give You Back Your Life, Time, & Sanity

Amy Motroni

©2025 All Rights Reserved. No portion of this book may be reproduced, stored in a retrieval system, or transmitted in any form or by any means—electronic, mechanical, photocopy, recording, scanning, or other—except for brief quotations in critical reviews or articles without the prior permission of the author.

Published by Game Changer Publishing

Paperback ISBN: 978-1-969372-61-2

Hardcover ISBN: 978-1-969372-62-9

Digital ISBN: 978-1-969372-63-6

www.GameChangerPublishing.com

For my amazing children and husband—without you, I would have never learned these game-changing tools that are now helping thousands of other moms.

Your love, support, and excitement for Genius Mom Hacks gave me the courage to keep going when I doubted myself. Each of you believed in me, and that belief has been my greatest motivation.

READ THIS FIRST

Just to say thank you for reading *Genius Mom Hacks,* I've put together an exclusive bonus to help you take action immediately. When you scan the QR code, you'll get instant access to my **Top 10 Stress-Slaying Checklist** and my **Sunday Reset Checklist**. These two checklists will jump-start creating effective routines that will transform your home and your life as a busy mom.

I can't wait to see how you start eliminating the stress caused by your home's chaos today!

Scan the QR Code Here:

GENIUS MOM HACKS
THE TOOLS AND ROUTINES THAT WILL GIVE YOU BACK YOUR LIFE, TIME, & SANITY

AMY MOTRONI

PRAISE FOR AMY MOTRONI

"As a fellow creator, I'm inspired by the way Amy helps moms put their homes on autopilot while involving the whole family. Her approach is practical and encouraging, and she has a way of making everyday life feel lighter. Amy has a true gift for simplifying home life. Her routines not only work, they inspire."

—Amanda Johnson, **@Allthingsnew_home**

"Amy is the real deal. She lives what she teaches and provides transformational tools for your home. As a mom of four kids, she gets it."

—Heather Mrak, **Baby's Best Brain**

"I found Amy on Instagram and was immediately drawn to her authenticity and genuineness. I learned so many incredible and helpful tips and habits from her free resources that it quickly became a no-brainer to get her guides.

Amy has created an incredible community and is leading the way in helping busy women transform their homes (and lives!) from overwhelming to peaceful and joyful.

What I love most about Amy is that she shares from a place of realness and vulnerability through her own personal journey. She understands the hardships of juggling motherhood, marriage, a home, and all the other responsibilities that come with life.

I don't say it lightly when I say that Amy's guides have changed my life."

—Olivia Pousseur, **Weight Loss Coach**

"I've had the privilege of watching Amy build her 'Genius Mom Hacks' brand from the ground up, and I can confidently say she is the real deal. What makes Amy stand out is not just her creativity and the systems she shares, but the heart behind her work. She deeply understands the challenges busy moms face and has a unique way of making home management feel approachable, doable, and even fun.

Amy lives what she teaches—her life reflects the very systems she shows others how to use. I've seen firsthand how her strategies free up mental space, time, and energy for her clients so they can focus on what matters most: their families. She is practical, compassionate, and a true encouragement to anyone feeling overwhelmed.

If you're looking for someone who doesn't just hand you tips but actually gives you the tools and confidence to create a home that runs on autopilot, Amy is that person. She has changed so many lives with her content, and I know her book will do the same."

—*Jenna Peterson*, **Online Business Coach**

"Amy's mission is so clear through all of her work: helping moms feel less stressed out by their homes! I'm often referring my clients to her work when they tell me their home is driving them nuts and they feel like they're going in circles!

Amy is practical and also empathetic—she meets people where they are and supports them toward their goals. It's incredible to witness!"

—*Rachael Choate*, **Mom Anger Coach**

"Amy's book is what every mom doesn't know she's missing. It's bursting with practical strategies and is easy to apply instantly at home. She keeps it simple but impactful and shows how to bring the whole family on board with her teamwork tips.

Best of all, she writes with honesty and vulnerability. Amy feels like me, like you. She's your best mom-friend, handing you the permission slip you've been waiting for. Whatever you're feeling in motherhood, this book says: it's OK."

— *Claire Muir*, **Little Black Dog Media**

CONTENTS

My Story — xi

1. What Didn't Work and Why That Matters — 1
2. Overcoming Mom Guilt and Unrealistic Expectations — 11
3. Routines That Rescue — 23
4. Redefining Productivity for Moms — 41
5. Creating a Functional Home Without the Fancy Bins — 55
6. Building Team Players in Your Home — 69
7. Independent Play and Smoother Mornings — 81
8. Finding My Identity Again — 97
9. The Bigger Picture: From Winging It to Walking in Wisdom — 103

Conclusion — 109
About Amy Motroni — 115

MY STORY

At the age of thirty-three, I found myself in the fetal position on my family room floor, wailing, with a two-year-old toddler and a three-month-old baby, spiraling, completely overwhelmed, hating motherhood, and wanting to walk away from it all.

This was way harder than I imagined. I had given up my career to be a mom, chosen to be a stay-at-home mom (SAHM), built a real estate business on the side, and thought I was walking into the best days of my life: motherhood.

But I was drowning. And it was nothing like I envisioned.

I was doing what every other mom was doing. I was winging motherhood. I even had a mug that said it. But everything felt hard and exhausting. How are other moms doing this?

I knew that motherhood wasn't supposed to feel like this, but I couldn't figure out where to start.

HOW I TRANSFORMED MY LIFE

I'll never forget the day when everything changed for me.

I was trying to put towels away in an overstocked linen closet with a baby on my hip and a toddler at my feet, and all the towels fell to the ground, unraveling right in front of me. All that work, wasted.

Immediately, I had feelings and thoughts of: *I hate being a mom. It's these kids that are making this feel so hard. If only my husband were home more.*

Every thought was blaming someone else or blaming my situation. None of it was helpful or provided a solution to get me out of my slump.

After a few minutes of just sitting in my feelings on the ground, something happened that transformed being a mom for me. I felt the need to look up. To look around my home. And for the first time, God gave me eyes to see my home for what it actually was.

I saw a home that was chaotic.

I saw dishes overflowing from the sink. I saw my table littered with papers and mail. I saw toys all over my family room. I saw laundry all over my couch. I saw my linen closet filled with so much stuff. I saw shoes piled by the front door and unfinished projects on the floor next to the office.

Every time before this moment, I would look at my home and tell myself, *This is what a home with young kids, toddlers, and babies looks like.* And it's true, managing a home with a baby and a toddler is busy from morning to evening, and the state of my home was justified. I was normal. My home was normal.

But here's the truth: it was costing me my stress, anxiety, time with my kids, and my entire motherhood.

But for the first time, I saw my stress wasn't coming from my kids, my husband, or my situation (full-time SAHM with a husband who worked a lot and commuted)... It was my *home*.

CHANGING MY LIFE DIDN'T HAPPEN OVERNIGHT

I would love to tell you that once I had my lightbulb moment, everything fell into place and I immediately felt lighter, that motherhood felt easier. That I was fixed.

Nope.

I actually didn't even know what to do first. So I started researching—listening to podcasts and reading blog posts. There was a lot to unpack in this new revelation.

I kept trying different things: ruthless decluttering, buying all the cute, fancy organizational bins, and creating huge, never-ending to-do lists. But even after completing a decluttering challenge, within a few weeks, the clutter returned.

The expensive baskets were useless if the toys always ended up on the floor instead of in the baskets. Those massive to-do lists only left me feeling more stressed and like a failure when I couldn't cross off every task.

While all of these tools were helpful and great places to start when trying to simplify my home, none of them taught me how to *maintain* a simplified home day in and day out. They didn't show me *how* to manage the endless laundry, constant cleaning, or nonstop meals. They weren't solving the root issues—just offering band-aid fixes.

HOW THIS BOOK WILL BENEFIT YOU

This book covers the missing tools in motherhood: what they are, why they work, and how they can help you eliminate your stress, create an easy-to-clean home on autopilot with a family that works together, and get two hours of uninterrupted kid-free time. These are the tools that I've used to go from being overwhelmed and hating being a mom to being in control and loving being a mom again!

You will learn that many of these tools are supported by science and are mind strategies. Motherhood is just as physical as it is mental, and we need to learn tools that can help in both areas.

Plus, you'll learn how to apply these concepts and tools to your own life and start seeing immediate results. These tools have already helped more than 10,000 moms, and I cannot wait for you to read this book and put them into practice.

If you can promise to see this book through to the end, you'll have a clear roadmap. And as Robin Sharma says in his book *The 5AM Club*, "Small changes, when done consistently over time, have huge results."

So let's get your home on autopilot with these *Genius Mom Hacks*.

HOW LIFE CAN LOOK WITH A HOME ON AUTOPILOT

Before we dive in, I want to share what my life looks like now, after years of practicing what I preach, so you can see upfront how these tools can transform your life too. I'll also share some impactful testimonials from students I've coached who achieved the same results.

MY STORY

It's been over eight years since I started this journey, and while it didn't happen overnight, I can proudly say I've eliminated the overwhelm and stress that plague most moms. I get hours of *me time* each week without relying on screens to occupy my kids. I've created a home I love that takes just minutes to clean each day, and my kids are team players who help, so I'm no longer Cinderella in my own home. I've escaped laundry prison by eliminating endless piles, and I have the energy to be an active, present mom. I get more done in less time, and my kids play independently for hours.

Wow. That's a lot.

For years, I thought the best thing was accomplishing this for myself. Well, it turns out the best thing is helping other stressed moms accomplish it for themselves!

In 2023, I created an online publication called *Genius Mom Hacks*, where I've been sharing these tools with the world. It's not only a blog with more than 100 posts but also a growing social media presence. The *Genius Mom Hacks* Instagram account took off in February 2024, and in the past year and a half, I've helped over 10,000 moms through my digital products.

Check out these three testimonials from real moms I've helped during that time. While I'm only sharing three, I actually have hundreds of inspiring stories.

MY STORY

This is **Olivia**: a business owner, busy mom of two, and eight months pregnant.

 On Amy, I have to tell you that this is literally what my house looks like EVERY SINGLE day since buying your guide!!!!
🩶

Edited

 This week I solo parented for 5 days, had an emergency ER visit AND am hosting for the weekend 😅 And it hasn't been stressful for one minute! I'm headed out for the day with my family and friends (my one load of laundry is in the washer) and my house is spotless 🩶 PS I have a 3 and 4 year AND my 3rd is due in 3 weeks 😅 WE CAN change our habits and create routines that stick and work! Thank you!
🩶

MY STORY

This is **Stephanie**: a business owner and busy mom.

steph.spencer.lindley 3h · ♥ by author
Game changer!!! Love your systems and courses, Amy 🔥🫶♥️✨ I've been a die hard messy girl my whole life and my husband who is super tidy is like, who are you?! You've seriously changed my life, not to be dramatic haha

This is **Rachael**: online mom coach and busy mom to three.

Amy!!! As I have been applying Genius Mom Hacks, I've seen where me doing it ALL is just NOT helpful. "Teamwork is Light Work" is the missing piece to introducing the concept of having a team spirit. I knewwww that there was something missing when I found myself saying, "I'm not the maid!" I realized I wasn't teaching my kids HOW to have a helpful heart and HOW to help. And I realized I was totally guilty of "being too specific" 🙈 that alone has been so helpful in allowing my kids to be more involved!!! Thank you for this!!

Today, I work from home while my kids are at school, sharing these tools with the world. And this job feels like a dream job.

After graduating from college, I worked as a business systems analyst and a technical project manager for ten years. I mention this because the skills I gained in those roles became the catalyst for getting my home on autopilot once I became a mom and the stress hit hard.

MY STORY

I married an amazing man at thirty, and within two years, we had our first son, Aiden. After Aiden was born, I left my corporate job to become a stay-at-home mom. I was fortunate to have built a real estate business, which allowed me to continue working from home while caring for him. Like most moms, I quickly realized that motherhood was nothing like I expected. But it wasn't until after I had my second son that I truly hit rock bottom and knew I needed to make a change.

Our home is still full of energy and noise. We got pregnant again and found out we were having *twins*! Hello! Now we have four kids, three active boys and one chatty Kathy daughter, but it's no longer the kind of chaos that feels chaotic. It's loud, it's busy, but it's not a stressful mess.

That shift didn't happen by accident. It happened because I built systems that supported me. Systems that work for me—not against me. I'm no longer drowning in laundry or stepping over toys just to make my morning coffee. My home runs on routines. Everyone in the house has a role to play, even the seven-year-old twins.

Teamwork is our family culture now, and I often thank myself for putting in the hard work in those younger years to have the fruit of my labor today. Mornings are smoother. My weekends aren't spent binge-cleaning, and I'm no longer collapsing in bed still feeling behind.

Now I get to be the present, active mom that I always hoped and wanted to be. I've built a business helping thousands of other moms do the same, but most importantly, I've built a home I love living in, one that feels like my sanctuary.

Our calendar is full these days, and I wouldn't want it any other way. Between sports practices and games for all four kids, church on Sundays, hosting midweek Bible studies, hosting life groups, volunteering in youth group, coaching kids' sports teams, and being the house where birthday parties, holiday gatherings, and spontaneous hangouts happen, our life is rich in activity and relationships. But here's the key difference: It's not running me ragged anymore. I can say *yes* to the things that matter to community, to connection, to being present for my kids because I'm no longer buried under the weight of a messy home and unmanageable mental load. I have capacity.

Routines are the invisible structure that holds everything together. I know when the laundry will get done. I know that, if the house gets messy, we have established daily resets to turn it around in minutes. I know what's for dinner, even when we're running from sports to more sports. My brain doesn't have to hold or remember these tiny details.

And that's only possible because of the systems I built, not because I figured out how to do more. These routines are what allow me to live a busy life without burnout.

When I first got pregnant, I felt pretty confident heading into motherhood. I had read a ton about sleep schedules and life with a newborn. Several of my friends and my sister already had babies, so I felt I knew a lot and was ready for that aspect. But no one was talking about the home management of being a mom. No one. I had no idea.

> And then I realized: I was never taught or given the tools to know how to manage my home. I assumed I would just know. Figure it out. How hard could it really be? Turns out, really hard!

After having my first baby, it took me a couple of years of blaming my kids before I realized it was my home.

And then I realized: I was never taught or given the tools to know how to manage my home. I assumed I would just know. Figure it out. How hard could it really be? Turns out, really hard!

MY STORY

I was very taken aback by the insane amount of work required to run and manage a household, especially once you start having kids and lots of kids, plus multiples. I had great sleepers and was regularly getting seven-plus hours of sleep. I kept telling myself, *It shouldn't be this hard. Why am I so stressed?*

My babies are great. I'm so lucky compared to other moms whose babies aren't sleeping through the night. But here I was, still short-tempered, easily agitated, annoyed with my kids, frustrated by everything that still needed to get done, exhausted, and stressed.

Looking back, I'm so thankful I had this huge lightbulb moment. It puts everything into perspective and makes it all so clear.

While on this journey, I read a study from Princeton that said, "Your environment directly relates to your stress levels."[1] That changed everything for me. It helped me understand that if my home was messy and chaotic, I would be more stressed. Period. I was able to see it in terms as black and white as that. And for me, that felt motivating, because now that I understood what was causing my stress, I could learn how to eliminate my stress.

This was something I hadn't heard or thought of before. I was trying so hard to be the perfect mom, but for the first time, it clicked: if I was less stressed about my home, I would have more capacity to be the mom I wanted to be—more patient, more involved, more fun.

I can't control my kids' emotions or responses, but I *can* control my home.

---

1. Brandi Silver, "Tidying Up Your Environment to Improve Your Mental Well-Being," *Burke County Center*, N.C. Cooperative Extension (3 January 2024), https://burke.ces.ncsu.edu/2024/01/tidying-up-your-environment-to-improve-your-mental-well-being/.

Science was proving it. I was *feeling* it. This was where I needed to start.

WHAT DID I LEARN FROM THIS JOURNEY?

I learned that many times, we try fixing our problems with Band-Aid fixes instead of root solutions. I realized that decluttering and organizing were just band-aid fixes. They didn't address the root issue. What finally brought lasting change were daily routines, anchors, productivity tools, and creating a functional home. These gave me the framework I needed to solve the deeper problem.

I used to be the mom who rarely sat down—not because I didn't want to, but because I couldn't. Every corner of my home had a mess waiting for me. I'd pick up the toys, only to trip over a laundry basket five minutes later. I always felt a mess needed my immediate attention, and I never felt like I made any progress in my home. Just spinning my wheels.

I couldn't remember the last time I drank my coffee hot, let alone sat down to enjoy it in peace and quiet. I was always behind. Behind on dishes. Behind on laundry. Behind on my mental to-do list. My mind never stopped running. I remember walking into the kitchen most mornings and feeling defeated before the day had even begun.

The counters were cluttered. The floors needed sweeping. I had no idea what we were going to eat. I didn't feel like the mom I wanted to be. I snapped at my kids—not because I didn't love them, but because I was exhausted, tapped out, and mentally maxed. Every little thing felt big because I had no margin. No breathing room. No capacity. No plan.

I truly believe God opened my eyes and helped me see my home for what it was: chaotic, messy, and a major source of stress.

MY STORY

My home wasn't supporting me. It wasn't functioning for our family.

It wasn't giving me the peace or clarity I so desperately needed. Instead, it was working against me—draining me, adding to my stress, frustration, and mental overload—until I had nothing left. Just clutter, chaos, and messes, with no end in sight.

The mental load of keeping everything ready, of constantly cleaning up the same messes, of never being able to find what I needed, was silently breaking me.

I realized I needed better tools. This wasn't about being a better mom or trying harder. It was about finally understanding that if I wanted to stop drowning, I needed to stop blaming myself and start building a home that helped me.

From that moment on, I became obsessed with finding systems, routines, and strategies that would make our home run more smoothly so that I could show up for my family without always feeling like I was falling apart. And the twins weren't even a thought at that time. That moment on the floor wasn't the end.

It was just the beginning.

One of the most common challenges moms face today is decision fatigue: the sheer number of daily decisions we're expected to make. And it's not just your load. You carry everyone else's too. And you're exhausted.

Then there's the overstimulation. So much information comes at you all day long that by the end of the day, your brain is fried.

Our nervous systems are often on high alert, constantly processing the needs of our children and the world around us. But when our sensory systems become overloaded, it's overwhelming and exhausting. Sensory overload happens when the brain receives more input than it can handle, leading to a feeling of overstimulation. For many moms, this happens when we try to do too much at once or when there's too much noise, bright light, or activity around us. It can leave us feeling tense, irritable, and even physically drained.

I started reading blogs, listened to countless podcasts, and devoured book after book. I was shocked at what I learned. For starters, society is screaming at moms that motherhood will always feel hard, stressful, and exhausting. Winging motherhood is portrayed as "normal," and "barely surviving" is idolized. We have influencers on social media constantly praising the version of motherhood that is messy and chaotic, throwing their hands up and telling us, 'This is life, just deal with it,' but providing no tools, solutions, or alternatives, all while living lives that most of us can't afford.

We live in a culture that screams materialism and overconsumption. We fall for the trap and are left with more stuff, more stress, and more chaos.

Yes, we feel seen. We don't feel alone. We think, *Thank goodness I'm not the only one*, but sitting in these thoughts does absolutely nothing to move us forward.

In the last decade or so, we've lost the handoff from mother to daughter: the passing down of knowledge about how to manage a home and the tools that once were carried through generations.

Not by my mom. Not in school. No one sat down and taught me how to run a household or build routines. I didn't know how to manage laundry for six people, how to meal plan, or how to clean without spending my entire weekend playing catch-up. One day, I blinked and found myself an adult, married with four kids (with twins), and completely hating motherhood.

I didn't have the tools. I didn't even know I needed tools. I just knew I didn't like this version of motherhood. This wasn't what I signed up for.

How did this happen? I think society changed faster than moms could keep up. What worked for them no longer worked for the next generation. Modern motherhood looks drastically different from what previous generations experienced. Most moms now work full-time outside the home, and there's a growing commitment to sports and extracurricular activities. For the first time in history, many moms entered motherhood without a village. They faced isolation, constant comparison, and no tools.

So many of my mom friends were winging motherhood and drowning in the chaos of their homes. They were barely surviving, just trying to get to the next season in one piece.

In my mom groups every mom was feeling and saying the same thing. Everyone felt heard, but no solutions were shared. We all just nodded and agreed that this was motherhood: it was hard, it was messy, it was exhausting, but this was the season we were in.

A cycle of martyrdom. It was comforting to know I wasn't the only one feeling that way, but at the same time, it was frustrating that no one had real solutions. I wanted solutions.

I needed real systems that worked for real moms with real kids in real homes that weren't always clean. Once I experienced a shift, I knew I couldn't keep it to myself.

Because here's what I know now: Too many moms are silently drowning in overwhelm, carrying the weight of a home they were never taught how to manage, blaming themselves for the chaos, thinking they're the problem.

I wrote this book for her: for the mom who's tired but trying; for the woman who wants a better way but doesn't know where to start; for the family that deserves more peace, more presence, and more joy.

MY STORY

This book is more than systems.

It's a roadmap to freedom. A reminder that you're not failing—you're just ready for something new. That's why I wrote this book: to hand you what I wish someone had handed me to say, "Here, try this."

Managing your home isn't a magic silver bullet. It requires intention. It requires knowing the right tools, putting in the work, mindset shifts, and making changes. It's a domino effect: not one big leap, but a series of small, daily shifts that, when done consistently, lead to huge results.

Yes, there will be hard seasons. And that's exactly why these systems and routines matter even more. I started making changes with a newborn and an active toddler—and soon after that, I had twins. Three boys. One girl. Multiples. Short age gaps. It was hard.

Motherhood is hard.

But this is about progress over perfection. If you change nothing, nothing changes.

And here's what you need to know: it works. And I'm so honored to show you. I don't have a spotless house or a picture-perfect life. I'm a real mom, just like you, who got tired of drowning in chaos and stress and decided something had to change.

I didn't write this book from a place of theory. I wrote it from experience: experience crying on the floor surrounded by laundry, yelling at my kids, and feeling crushed with guilt, running a home and raising four kids, and realizing that winging it was costing me my peace and my joy.

I didn't find some magical solution. This journey was full of trial and error.

What started with one changed home has become a growing community of over 10,000+ moms who are reclaiming calm and creating homes that work. I'm not perfect—I don't pretend to be.

MY STORY

But I've lived this transformation. And if it worked for me, it can work for you too.

Inside these pages, you'll discover what's truly possible when you stop winging it and start building a home that runs on autopilot.

At the heart of this book are five core pillars that changed everything for me and for the thousands of moms I've helped through *Genius Mom Hacks*:

1. Routines that run the home
2. Productivity tools that save you time
3. Creating team players in your kids
4. Progress over perfection
5. Functional over organized

Together, these pillars give you the foundation to eliminate the stress caused by the chaos in your home. You'll learn how to create a home that feels lighter, functions better, and supports your family without draining you.

When you turn the final page, I hope you feel a shift within: not pressure to change everything at once, not shame for what's been hard, but a deep, steady sense of hope and motivation.

Hope that your home can feel different.

Motivation to take action and make the changes needed so that motherhood feels lighter.

And knowing that you don't have to do it perfectly to do it well.

I hope you feel less alone and more in control. I hope you feel seen, supported, and equipped. I hope you stop winging motherhood and begin walking forward with tools in hand.

Let me be clear: I got here the hard way, through trial and error, frustration, tears, and a whole lot of progress over perfection.

The truth is, before things got better, I had to get honest. I had to face the reality that no one was coming to save me. No one was going to solve this or figure it out for me—it was up to me. I could either sit in that feeling forever or get up and do something about it. I chose to be the CEO of my home, and you can too.

So, let's dive in.

CHAPTER 1
WHAT DIDN'T WORK AND WHY THAT MATTERS

Once I realized that it was my home causing me stress and not my kids (or husband), I went searching for solutions. I read blog posts, listened to podcasts, and spent hours on Pinterest trying to see what the experts suggested I do first. I was committed to the journey of transforming my home.

When I looked around, all I saw was clutter and a mess. Toys were scattered across the floor. Papers covered the dining room table. The kitchen sink and counters were filled with dishes and leftovers from the night before. It finally became clear just how much my home was contributing to my stress.

The first thing that came to mind was to declutter. I could see all the extra stuff we had—the disorganization, the clutter, the chaos. I thought, *That's what I need to do,* and I began a ruthless decluttering process.

I embarked on a journey that spanned multiple weekends, purging everything I could. I tackled the linen closets, cabinets, and any other space that held things we didn't need.

I literally grabbed big black trash bags and started tossing stuff in. I believed that if I could just get the stuff out, I could fix the chaos. I truly felt that the clutter was the root of my overwhelm.

I spent hours purging drawers, closets, and toy bins, chasing that peaceful, Pinterest-worthy home. It wasn't an overnight transformation; it took me a few weeks. But once I had scraped the surface and cleared out so much unnecessary stuff, it felt amazing.

I could finally breathe again. It felt freeing.

But then, I was shocked. Within a month, I felt weighed down and stressed all over again. The stuff had come back. The mess had returned.

We live in a materialistic world, and it was naive of me to think one big decluttering session would solve everything. Because as I was getting things out of the house, more things were coming in—especially as our family grew.

Looking back, I don't regret purging anything. I was hyper-focused on clearing the clutter.

I looked at my kids' toys and purged at least 50 percent of them. Several of my friends and my sister had already had kids and no longer needed baby equipment or toys, so I ended up with a ton of hand-me-downs. I was so grateful for their generosity, and as a first-time mom, I said yes to almost everything: multiple swings, bouncers, and more. We knew we wanted more than one child, and I didn't yet know what we'd actually need.

Now I realize we had way too much baby gear, toys, and equipment. It took up every inch of our home: closets, bedrooms, bathrooms, the family room, all packed with things I thought we might need. Instead of moving one bouncer between rooms, I had two, one for each. We had so many toys, many of them battery-operated and rarely played with. They were bulky and took up so much space.

It was a classic first-time mom mistake. My kids didn't need all that stuff. Letting go of each item felt like lifting a weight off my shoulders. At the time, I was convinced decluttering would solve all my problems. And for a month or so, it felt like it had. But the stuff crept back in. I realized that ruthless decluttering was a helpful tool, but not a long-term solution. It didn't eliminate my stress and chaos for good. What I was missing was a routine: a system to stay on top of the daily mess and the constant flow of new stuff coming in.

At that point, we hadn't had the twins yet. Now, looking back, I see how short-sighted it was to think one decluttering spree would solve everything. With kids constantly attending birthday parties, bringing home school projects, and celebrating holidays, there's a never-ending stream of stuff entering the home.

A single Saturday of ruthless decluttering—spending eight hours clearing things out and donating them—can feel amazing. But it won't bring lasting results unless you create a system to manage the everyday inflow. Otherwise, you'll always be relying on ruthless decluttering to keep your home manageable. More Amazon packages show up at our front door than visitors stopping by to say hi.

I wish I'd realized sooner that we weren't managing or staying on top of all the stuff. But I had to go through the trial-and-error process to figure out what didn't work before I discovered what did.

Spoiler alert: The real issue was that I lacked consistent, effective daily routines and systems to manage my home (and life as a busy mom).

> Spoiler alert: The real issue was that I lacked consistent, effective daily routines and systems to manage my home (and life as a busy mom).

We'll get to all of that soon, the things that actually worked. But first, let's talk about the second thing I tried that didn't work. Because maybe you're doing it right now and wondering why you're still overwhelmed and stressed.

After graduating from college with a degree in Business Management and Marketing, I got a job right away as a business systems analyst. I loved it. It taught me so much, like how to write (hello, five guides and one book later!), how to manage tasks, create lists, and think analytically. From there, I moved into a technical project management role, handling large enterprise technical projects.

I thrive on lists. Naturally, I started using them to manage everything about "mom life" and running a home. That's why I was shocked when I realized my sticky note lists weren't working for me anymore as a busy mom. Lists work great when your environment and schedule are controllable. But motherhood isn't like that. You can't control the variables.

In my job, I would walk into my office and set the tone for the day, for the most part. I used lists, calendaring tools, and time blocking to manage my schedule. I could control interruptions and plan meetings in ways that worked for me. While work always had its share of fire drills and unexpected issues, it was nothing like motherhood.

And when there were interruptions, they weren't from children. They were adult interruptions, people I could reason with and manage using adult conversations.

But then I became a stay-at-home mom with two kids who didn't care about my intentions or plans for the day. They didn't speak or reason like adults, and my day was constantly thrown off course. My long to-do list failed me day in and day out.

That list didn't account for explosive diapers, random emergency trips to the doctor's office, or a toddler just having a bad attitude that day. Suddenly, I couldn't run the errand I had planned because there was no way I was taking a cranky, tantrum-throwing toddler to the store. Or maybe one of the kids was sick, and we just needed to stay home and keep things calm.

So, I thought I needed to get better at making my to-do lists. I like lists. They're comforting. I love the feeling of checking things off. As someone who thrives on lists, I was hopeful they would help me through this season of motherhood. But the problem with long to-do lists in motherhood is that you must filter everything through the lens of being a mom. Your time is limited, you've got less emotional bandwidth, and interruptions are constant.

To-do lists work great in other seasons of life. But once I became a mom, with a newborn and a toddler, so much of the day became unpredictable. You simply can't plan your day the way you used to. Lists often don't account for the flexibility you need.

They're often unrealistic, a brain dump of everything we want to get done that day or week. There's no consideration of timeframes or priorities. We rarely look at the list and assess what's actually achievable. Instead, it becomes a source of stress and self-judgment.

The list doesn't help with the mental load either. Your brain still tries to figure out when you'll do the task and how long it will take. Instead of reducing stress, it adds to it. We get frustrated and angry with ourselves when items don't get crossed off. Lists left me feeling defeated, resentful, and like a constant failure.

Every unchecked box became proof that I wasn't doing enough. My home didn't feel like it was making progress. Even the motivation to check the boxes wasn't enough to get the results I wanted. And that really frustrated me.

So now what do I do?

After trying decluttering and long to-do lists, I thought, *Maybe I just need to be more organized.* If my home were more organized, maybe I'd feel calmer and less stressed. I was going to get all those pretty Pinterest-style bins and containers with fun labels and create a perfectly organized home.

I went on Pinterest and found all the pretty organization hacks.

I launched into an organizing spree. Everything needed a cute bin or a container. And in the end, yes, I had a lot of beautiful baskets…but no one was putting things back in them. Stuff was still getting left out, and my home was still stressing me out.

The bins looked great, but they weren't functional. They weren't in the right places. My home looked organized, but it wasn't easy to manage or clean.

I didn't find the peace I was hoping for. I was still overwhelmed.

Sure, it worked for a minute. Getting similar things grouped together helped. But I realized that organization doesn't equal functionality. I had reduced clutter, and my home looked nice, but it still wasn't easy to manage with two kids aged three and two.

When you have small children and you want them to help, functionality becomes more important than aesthetics. I didn't understand that at first. I wouldn't have known this unless I'd gone through the whole exercise of organizing my entire home and still not finding the peace, stress relief, or mental clarity I had hoped for.

I still felt burned out, like I was chasing a moving target.

What I did learn was that you don't need a prettier home; you need a more functional one. That's when I stopped trying to do what should work and started building what actually does work. What does work is building systems and routines that create lasting results in your home.

Later in this book, I'll dive deeper into what a functional home really means. But first, I want to explain the difference between an organized home and a functional home so you understand why this matters.

An organized home has all your stuff tucked away in baskets. You might not see messes on the floor or countertops, but if you open a drawer or cabinet, it's hard to quickly find what you're looking for. Items may not be where you want or need them; they're hidden out of sight, not eliminated or streamlined.

Many people organize their homes like the infamous "miscellaneous drawer" in the kitchen. They throw a bunch of vaguely related things into a basket and call it good. But when you go to find something, it takes forever, and it's frustrating. That's not functional.

If you can't quickly see what's inside a basket or easily access everything in it, then all you've done is hide the clutter.

You're still left digging through piles of stuff, just now inside a container. That's not solving anything; it's simply a prettier form of disorganization.

A functional home still uses organizational tools like baskets. (I'm a big fan. I talk more about them later in the book. I especially love Lazy Susans because they allow you to see everything at a glance.) But in a functional home, it's easy to find what you need and access it quickly. Everything has a purpose and a place, and it's in the right place at the right time.

Here's a simple example. You're in the kitchen, and your child spills Cheerios on the floor. In a functional home, there's a broom conveniently stored next to the counter. The mess is cleaned up in thirty seconds. Or maybe there are baby wipes stored in a drawer right by the island: no stress, no delay.

Here's the truth: we often tell ourselves, *When the kids are older…* or *In the next season of life, things will be easier.* And while it's true that motherhood changes as kids grow, and some aspects do become easier, if you want a change, you have to make it.

I waited for a long time. I was waiting for someone to save me. Waiting for my kids to get older. But those seasons feel long when you're stuck and overwhelmed. And they can feel never-ending when you're just enduring rather than changing.

Don't wait.

Don't wait for the next season. Don't expect someone else to fix it. Learn the tools now. Take charge of your home and your life. That's where transformation starts.

I remember sitting on the floor, crying, looking around my house, and having that lightbulb moment. I told myself: *I'm done. I'm done living like this.*

I decided to do whatever it took to see the change I wanted. I stopped waiting for someone to save me. I had built up so much resentment toward my husband, thinking if only he were around more, helped more, did certain things better, then I wouldn't feel this way.

I kept thinking, *If only my kids and husband were different, then my home would feel less chaotic. Then I'd enjoy motherhood more. I wouldn't feel so angry, resentful, and bitter.*

That mindset? That's looking for someone else to save you. You have to be honest with yourself. Realize that nothing changes if you change nothing. That's what brings real freedom.

I went from working full-time to being a full-time stay-at-home mom doing part-time real estate from home. My husband was growing his career, so I was home a lot.

I expected that when he came home, he'd take over and I could be "off." But that's not how it worked. He was coming home after ten-hour days, and we were both exhausted, both expecting more from each other. The rhythm and routine I had created with the kids wasn't something he could just step into. That disconnect caused tension and resentment. I was trying to eliminate stress in our home with new routines and systems, but he didn't immediately understand or support those changes. It felt like he was adding to the stress.

Eventually, we got there. But I kept working to build a teamwork-based home. I was teaching our kids to be more independent, setting up systems so everyone could pitch in. It took time, but we got there.

That's why I want moms to learn these tools early. Start implementing them now. The sooner you do, the sooner you'll get your family working together.

Having honest conversations with your spouse or partner and inviting them into this journey is essential. Your home is the foundation of your family dynamic. It should be a place where you thrive, not just survive.

Getting honest with myself was the start. Realizing that I had to make the effort. Ruthless decluttering, long to-do lists, and buying pretty organizing bins weren't the ultimate answer. But they were starting points that led me to what actually helped reduce my stress and put my home on autopilot.

Sometimes, you have to fail before you succeed.

In the end, I realized I didn't need a prettier home. I needed a home that served me. A home that took less time to clean. A home that was a sanctuary, not a source of stress.

CHAPTER 2
OVERCOMING MOM GUILT AND UNREALISTIC EXPECTATIONS

We all feel this in motherhood. As soon as you give birth and the baby is in your arms, you're already feeling that mom guilt.

And then, in different seasons, it hits so hard: the need for validation, the need to look like you have it all together. Chasing that clean home. Wishing it could look effortless. Believing that if it looked easy, maybe you'd finally feel like a good mom—not just in your own eyes, but in the eyes of everyone watching.

There's so much pressure to do everything perfectly. These days, it feels like moms keep adding hats to the roles we already carry.

The pressure and the expectations can feel debilitating and exhausting, and they can steal your joy. I know there were definitely seasons when they stole mine. Seasons when I hated motherhood.

My husband was excelling in his career, and I looked around and didn't even recognize who I was becoming. I had a completely different vision of what I thought motherhood would be. I had no idea the toll it would take or the weight of the role of managing a home.

One of the biggest unrealistic expectations we place on ourselves is the idea that we should naturally know how to run a household. I grew up with a stay-at-home mom. Our home was always tidy, decorated, and put together. So I assumed that once I got married and had kids, I would naturally do the same.

But somehow, watching my parents manage our home didn't translate into knowing how to do it myself. Honestly, I don't think I was ever really taught. I vividly remember seeing my mom and dad cleaning. I even helped. But once I became an adult, it was like none of it transferred. I had done the chores, but I hadn't learned how to do them on my own.

So there I was, sitting in my messy house with two young kids, drowning in mom guilt. Social media constantly showed me the "Pinterest mom": the one with homemade snacks, a color-coded pantry, beautifully decorated playrooms, spotless kitchens, and kids who never threw tantrums. Always smiling. Always calm. I was not that mom.

I remember being in mom groups, especially after the twins were born, and people would ask, "How's it going?" I was honest. I'd say, "It's not great. It's hard. I'm struggling. My kids are throwing tantrums, and I feel embarrassed taking all four of them out in public."

People would look at me with wide eyes and say, "You've got your hands full." Their gawking looks only added to the feeling that I didn't have it together, when I so desperately wanted to be the mom who looked like she did.

Motherhood was not going how I thought it would. I wanted to be the mom who loved motherhood, who loved being a mom, who was present and active in her kids' lives. But the truth was, my home was taking a serious toll on me.

Even as I began the first part of my journey toward getting my home on autopilot (spoiler alert: I do get there eventually), I kept striking out at first. It was hard not to think, *Maybe this just isn't possible.*

But what I finally realized was this: Supermom doesn't exist.

I wanted moms to know that motherhood can be hard. That you can have moments when you don't like being a mom and still be a great mom. Because there is more to motherhood than perfection. And no one has perfect days every day.

I remember thinking all the time: *I should be able to do this without help. I should be grateful—other moms have it harder. I'm blessed with four healthy children. I was able to give birth to all four. Many women pray for that. We got pregnant easily. And we even had twins naturally—fraternal twins.*

So it's genetics within my family. I am a twin who had twins. I felt like sometimes, when I wasn't enjoying seasons of being a mom or I was angry with my kids, I could feel shame in the fact that I wasn't being grateful because other people have different stories where they're not able to have kids, or their journey was different. You can start to beat yourself up for feeling that way.

I remember one moment in particular. My toddler was playing with wooden trains in the family room and asked me to come play with him. I was just a few feet away, folding laundry on the couch. My newborn was in a swing nearby. I smiled and nodded. I said, "One second."

And I realized I was saying "one second" a lot during that season when my home felt chaotic, when I felt like there was never enough time in the day, and when I had so many things I needed or wanted to get done. And that "one second" would turn into one minute, then thirty minutes, then another task that pulled me away.

I wasn't present. I wasn't choosing him. I wasn't soaking in those precious childhood moments like I wanted to. The housework was stealing the joy of being the present mom I longed to be.

That became my why.

So now, when I talk with moms or coach them through my systems, helping them get their homes on autopilot and their lives back so they can enjoy motherhood again, I always ask: "What is your *why*? Why do you want to do this?"

My kids are my why. I didn't want to keep telling them "one second." I wanted to be present and engaged in their lives—in that moment—not distracted by the endless mental load and the never-ending list of house tasks that always seemed to take priority.

I wanted to have more patience so I wasn't snapping at my kids all morning and all day long. Those reasons became my anchors and foundation. Knowing your why is the foundational anchor for change.

But it wasn't just about being a more present and active mom. I also wanted to reclaim time for rest, enjoyment, and rediscovering my identity. Before becoming a stay-at-home mom, I had a career, hobbies, and passions. But those things quickly took a back seat. My time and energy became all about the kids and the home, and I had no downtime to pour back into myself. That needed to change.

Looking back, I had a very present and active dad. My mom was a stay-at-home mom, and my dad worked a lot, but when he was home, he was present and available. He always said yes. If I asked him to come play basketball outside or play a board game, he always said yes.

After having kids of my own, I reflected on that a lot. It became a foundational memory I carry with me. To this day, my dad is still an active and involved papa. He's amazing with my kids: he's at every sports game, every school performance. And he still says yes, even as a Papa.

I wanted to be able to say yes too, without feeling like I'd pay for it later with a mountain of housework. I wanted to say yes because I had the time, the energy, and the capacity. Because nothing else needed my immediate attention.

Today, there are so many days when I look around my home and realize there's nothing that needs to be done. I can be the present, active mom I always wanted to be.

My home runs itself on autopilot. Saying yes is easy now, because I'm not weighed down by unfinished tasks. Even while running a business from home, I'm able to manage my home and still be the yes mom I wanted to become.

But let me be clear: it didn't happen overnight. I've been on this journey for eight years. Still, I believe if I had these tools from the very beginning, I would've gotten here so much faster.

At the beginning, I was hell-bent on figuring out how I could be highly active and present, even as a busy mom. I didn't know the twins were coming, but if I couldn't be an active and present mom to two, then how was I supposed to be with four?

So figuring all that out before the twins came was such a blessing I didn't even know I needed, and I'm so thankful. This journey was filled with many potholes, turns, and pivots. You're allowed to try something new, realize that it isn't working, and then do something different.

I had tried three different things that society told me would solve my problems, and none of them were the real solution for me: ruthless decluttering, creating massive to-do lists, and relying on cute, trendy organizational bins.

But here's the truth: you create the path.

Don't be afraid to try something new—something no one else is talking about. Because eight years ago, when I started this journey, moms weren't talking about effective routines, productivity tools, cleaning hacks, or setting up a home to actually function. Honestly, the most common message out there was just "winging motherhood."

There were no tools. There was no manual. Sleep schedules and sleep training were judged if you followed them, and independent play wasn't something anyone was even mentioning, let alone teaching.

I didn't care. I was determined to do what worked, not what was popular.

Success in motherhood isn't about crafting the perfect day. It's not about being the mom who never raises her voice, whose house always smells like fresh-baked cookies, or who never forgets a field trip form or spirit day outfit. (And seriously, why do we have spirit day? To this day, I still can't keep up. I am not the "spirit day" mom.)

I went from chaos to calm, from stress to peace, from surviving to thriving. I started thinking outside the box and doing things that other moms weren't doing or talking about. I focused on building routines, rhythms, and systems that actually worked for *me*.

Success, to me, is this:

- Waking up with a calm mind, not a chaotic one.
- Being able to show up with patience and love, even on the hard days.
- Creating a home that supports your family, not someone else's expectations.
- Teaching my kids that peace doesn't come from perfection, it comes from presence.

And honestly, one of the biggest things I pour into my family is teamwork.

Everyone plays a role. We all work together. We're present with each other, building memories and creating meaningful experiences. But it can feel impossible to work together as a team if your home is constantly in chaos.

During the early years, one of the hardest realities I faced was the sheer number of hours I spent home alone with my kids. I was a stay-at-home mom, holding down the fort so my husband could focus on his career. He was climbing the ladder—which was a good thing for our family—but it came with a long commute and long hours.

That meant I was home all day, every day, with four young kids.

Some days, it felt like I had lived twelve hours before it was even noon. I was juggling all the meals, naps, diaper changes, tantrums—and everything in between. It was relentless. There was no one to tag in, no one to help me. I remember so many nights folding laundry, completely exhausted, knowing I had to wake up and do it all over again.

That season was pivotal. I knew I didn't want to stay stuck. I needed to work smarter, not harder.

That time taught me how to build a home that could function even when I was the only one managing it. If you feel like everything falls on your shoulders, like it all rests on you, and your husband works long hours providing for the family (if you know, you know).

The right routines and systems can help your home run on autopilot. Because today, my home is my sanctuary. It's my favorite place to be. And I definitely would not have said that eight years ago when I was just starting out.

A lot of people like to say, "Well, your kids are older now." But it has *nothing* to do with the age of your children. It has everything to do with the systems that I built. And I started all of this when I stopped trying to be perfect, and I stopped trying to do what everyone else was doing and just focused on what was working for me and my family.

When I was putting away those towels, I fell to the ground, and one of the most significant things that happened in that moment was that I felt like God was opening my eyes and showing me something for the first time, something I had never seen before.

It was an "aha" moment, a brand-new revelation. I truly believe God was in that moment. I'm forever thankful because I feel like He's been on this journey with me the whole time.

When I looked around and saw my home for what it was, I realized I had never seen it that way before. It was like I was looking at the same home, but through a completely new lens. And it was those new lenses that shifted everything for me.

One of the biggest outcomes from that moment, especially related to creating the routines that have become so important in motherhood, was establishing a more consistent morning quiet time. Before I had routines, I would wake up to a baby crying or a toddler telling me he was hungry. I would wait until the last possible moment to roll out of bed, then hit the ground running, immediately focusing on the needs of my children.

One of the first changes I made in regard to creating new routines was to start waking up before my kids so I could set the tone for the day. I felt God showing me that to get through the day, I needed to be intentional, and that needed to start with Him.

So I began moving my body and starting my mornings with prayer and a quiet time. I love that God showed me the state of my home and used that to draw me closer to Him.

I say this all the time: Something done is better than nothing done. Don't get trapped by decision paralysis. In my career as a project manager and business systems analyst, it was easy to get caught up in perfection—so caught up in trying to make the right decision that no real progress was made. I think we do the same thing in motherhood: we strive for perfection. And in doing so, if something can't be perfect, we either don't try at all or we give up. That's the all-or-nothing mindset.

But something finished, even imperfectly, is more valuable than something perfect that never gets done. It's about lowering the bar, and that mindset is incredibly helpful in a season where time, energy, and sleep are all limited. When you have kids, and your sleep, energy, and time are drastically reduced, your expectations should be, too. We become moms, and suddenly we're tired, stretched thin, and carrying more responsibility, yet we often don't adjust our expectations. One of the mottos I live by is: Something done is better than nothing done. Focus on progress over perfection. Imperfect action will take you further than striving for perfection and doing nothing at all.

One of the most beautiful outcomes of lowering your expectations, throwing out the long to-do list, and getting hyper-focused on what truly moves the needle in your home is that it gives you freedom: freedom to say yes, freedom of time, freedom of mind. You gain the capacity to be a present, active mom. Your kids get to see you manage the home and still prioritize them. They thrive in that.

For me, this has been transformational in my relationship with my kids. They love that I'm a present mom: riding bikes, playing board games, card games, softball, wiffle ball, and football. Those are the memories I want them to carry with them. I believe that's the kind of mom most kids long for. They don't care about the to-do list. But if you fold your kids into a teamwork-centered home, two powerful things happen:

1. You get more done in less time.
2. They become part of managing the home.

You work together, and then you play together. I'll go deeper into this later, but let me say now: you were never meant to manage the entire home by yourself.

Another lie we tell ourselves as moms is that we're supposed to do it all, and that children should "just be children." And while I agree emotionally they should be allowed to just be, kids are far more capable than we give them credit for. And they want to help.

If you've ever met a toddler, you know they want to be involved. No, they won't do it perfectly. Yes, it may not meet your standards. But if you release perfection and invite them into your day-to-day life, they'll thrive, and they'll get better.

One of the most beautiful things about involving kids in the home is that it requires you to lower your expectations. And often, it's those expectations that keep them from joining you. You think, *I'll just fold this laundry myself. It's faster. I'll do it better. I don't need help.* But what you should be saying is: "Absolutely—come fold this laundry with me." Show them how. Work as a team. And when the task is done, go do something fun together.

One of the biggest benefits of getting your home on autopilot of creating an easy-to-clean, easy-to-maintain space, is that it's not about perfection (as I've said many times). It's about freeing yourself so you can show up better for your kids. You can't be fully present for them if you're constantly stressed and running on empty. You need that extra capacity to be patient, loving, and understanding, especially on the days when they test your patience the most.

Realizing that the majority of my stress came from my home allowed me to take a step back and see the bigger picture. Chances are, there's something in your environment contributing to your stress. Now when I catch myself losing patience or yelling at my kids, I pause and ask: *What's going on around me that's causing this reaction?*

This isn't about perfect motherhood. There are still moments when I yell or get it wrong. But now, I go back and apologize. I say, "I was short-tempered, but it wasn't really about you. It was the full sink of dishes, the tight time constraint, and the long to-do list. I felt overwhelmed and snapped, and I'm sorry."

Realizing that it was my home, not my kids or my circumstances, that was the root of my stress has been the most powerful insight of motherhood for me. For a long time, I blamed everything else: my kids, my husband's schedule, my situation. I used those things to justify my anger or poor responses.

But that wasn't the real reason.

Now I know I can show up with more love and intention because I finally understand why it matters.

CHAPTER 3
ROUTINES THAT RESCUE

So now let's talk about what actually worked for me and why you're really here.

I was a busy mom with a baby and a toddler (eighteen months apart) before I had the twins. I've now realized it was my home causing me stress. But after three failed attempts, I really started to wonder if anything was going to help.

I was bingeing podcasts and reading every mom blog I could find. And it was actually on a podcast where I came across the concept of routines. She was a mom who had just decluttered and purged more than 50 percent of her home and was sharing her journey about routines.

As soon as I heard the concept explained, I knew this was going to change my life forever. This was the missing piece I needed. It just made sense.

I immediately started experimenting with routines.

But why routines? What made me so excited about trying them? Here's what I learned and what I can now attest to after using them consistently for eight-plus years in every aspect of my life.

> Routines are easier for your brain. Things become autopilot. They become second nature, something we automatically do once the habit is built.

Routines are easier for your brain. Things become autopilot. They become second nature, something we automatically do once the habit is built.

This is important as a busy mom because you'll use less brain energy, and tasks will naturally feel easier and get done with minimal effort. Routines help you create habits, which bring a natural flow to your day. Without routines, your day will feel chaotic, stressful, and unorganized. If you have an area in your life that seems unorganized, like piles of laundry or dishes everywhere, you need a routine built in for those specific tasks. Routines save brainpower and allow you to function on autopilot. And anytime we can make motherhood feel easier and get more done in less time, it's a big win.

I started making small, manageable changes to my home. I created easy-to-follow routines. And I've been amazed at how they helped me eliminate stress and run my home in a way that now only takes minutes a day to maintain. When you save brainpower, you can use that energy on more important things and decisions. The results were far more impactful than I ever expected. If you don't have routines, you'll get overwhelmed more often because your brain is constantly having to think, *What's next? What should I do with this item?* or *Where should this item go?*

THE FIRST ROUTINE THAT CHANGED EVERYTHING

The first routine I started with was a morning routine. At that time, my mornings felt like a dumpster fire: a baby crying, a hungry toddler, a messy kitchen, and a to-do list that made me feel like a failure. My mornings were reactive instead of peaceful. I was rushing to find clean clothes, scrambling to figure out breakfast, and I never drank my coffee hot. After the third reheat in the microwave, I would give up.

It definitely didn't happen overnight, and I didn't start with twenty things I wanted to change. I came across Robin Sharma's book *The 5AM Club*, and this quote has been pivotal for me: "Small daily, seemingly insignificant improvements, when done consistently over time, yield staggering results." So I did exactly that. I slowly added new things to my morning routine.

The more detailed my morning routine became, the better I felt, and that was the fuel to keep going. Before I knew it, my chaotic mornings became peaceful and calm, even with a baby and toddler. That was the proof I needed to stay committed.

Before, I was going to bed late and waking up exhausted. I wasn't a priority. My health wasn't a priority. My mental health wasn't a priority. And it showed in how I showed up for my kids. Fast forward a few months of focusing on an effective morning routine, and now my husband brings me coffee in bed. He wakes up earlier than I do, so he gets us both coffee and brings it back to our room, where we start the day together, mostly in quiet. We sit in bed and either read, check our phones, or just stare out the window as the sun begins to rise. As he gets ready for work, we chat, and then I begin my morning routine to get ahead of the day before the kids wake up.

My morning routine is less than forty-five minutes and includes a mix of self-care, house chores, and productivity, three key elements to a successful day. To start the day ahead, rather than behind, is game-changing as a busy mom.

Before the kids have a chance to destroy the family room, I get to sit in it and enjoy it for a few quiet minutes. Before the kitchen gets messy with three meals and endless snacks, I start with an empty sink. To avoid drowning in laundry, I start one load a day.

Effective routines are designed to help you. They can be tailored to your personality and lifestyle. They should be flexible, leaving room to change with the seasons. Routines allow your day to flow and transition naturally from one thing to the next.

You don't want to cut and paste someone else's routine into your life. You want a routine that's for you, personally designed to fit your needs. That's why they work. That's why they stick: they are specific to where you are in life.

The first routine that rescued me, that truly brought relief, was a simple morning routine. I now drink my coffee hot, in peace and quiet. I knew how I started my day would directly impact the rest of my day. Yet I was starting my day with a crying baby and a whiny toddler. Immediately, I was in fight-or-flight mode, waking up already stressed. And when you start your day with that kind of adrenaline and energy, you're telling your brain and body: *We're in fight-or-flight mode today*. Already behind. Already overwhelmed. And that kind of energy is hard to reverse.

So I asked myself: *What do I need to do each morning so the rest of my day feels lighter, easier, and more peaceful?*

With a three-month-old and a toddler, I had to be strategic about using that time. What could I do to make my day easier? To set myself up for success before the day even started?

- Make my bed.
- I started one load of laundry (OLAD: One Load A Day).
- I emptied the dishwasher I had loaded the night before.
- I did a five-minute tidy of the main living areas.
- I squeezed in a fifteen-minute workout.

When I first started, I used the elliptical, which I'd moved from the garage into my bedroom. It wasn't aesthetic or pretty, but it worked. Aesthetics can wait. Functionality trumps.

Having the elliptical in my room meant I wouldn't wake the kids, and it made working out super easy. Just wake up, put on workout clothes (or don't. It's only you in your own room), hop on the elliptical, and then jump in the shower. All within thirty minutes.

This small shift created massive results. For the first time in forever, my house didn't feel like it was falling apart by 9 a.m. I wasn't waking up to screaming kids. I wasn't stepping on toys. I had laundry going. My sink was clean. My bed was made. And it wasn't even 7:30 a.m.

I was making myself a priority, something that had been pushed to the back burner in just two short years of motherhood.

THE DEEPER IMPACT OF ROUTINES

One of the best things about routines is how they allow you to make yourself a priority again.

Motherhood is mostly managing your thoughts. It's mental. And the best way to manage your mindset is to feed yourself first thing in the morning with helpful and encouraging words and move your body to stimulate energy and confidence.

Now I feel calmer. I'm not reacting. I'm not drowning. I'm starting to thrive. I can be more present with my kids instead of spiraling about everything that isn't getting done.

This routine worked when others failed because it was:

- Realistic
- Flexible
- Short
- Tied to my actual pain points
- Not dependent on my mood or how "good" I felt as a mom
- Simple and repeatable
- Rooted in progress, not perfection

You'll see that theme of progress over perfection again and again in my story.

The morning routine became my anchor. It didn't fix everything overnight, but it gave me my first real win. And from that win, I started to believe that maybe this is possible: Maybe I can manage my home and my peace with small steps that work.

After the success of my morning routine, I slowly started adding more. Once I nailed one routine, I'd add another. The next simple one was an evening routine. Instead of putting the kids down and crashing on the couch to binge Netflix until way past my bedtime, I'd spend fifteen minutes closing down the common areas.

So the next morning, I'd wake up to a clean home, not chaos.

After the kids were in bed, I'd:

- Pick up any toys left out
- Prep the coffee
- Wipe down the kitchen and counters
- Put dinner leftovers away
- Start the dishwasher

What I thought would feel like a chore ended up feeling therapeutic. And eight-plus years later, I still do both of these routines every single day.

Walking into a clean kitchen the next morning feels like a gift from my past self, and it makes me smile. It lights me up and makes me excited to start the day.

> Walking into a clean kitchen the next morning feels like a gift from my past self, and it makes me smile. It lights me up and makes me excited to start the day.

How I feel is everything in motherhood. I've walked into my kitchen in the early morning, with the sunlight hitting just right, and the peace I feel in that moment makes my home feel like a sanctuary. I turn on calm Christian music on my Apple Music, and my kids are all asleep. It's quiet. It is the most serene sanctuary moment that I think can exist within motherhood. With four kids, knowing that loudness is coming, I soak up these moments all the more.

And I just feel like so many moms are missing this moment. And you cannot think that you will not be changed by having that be your morning every morning versus a toddler screaming at you. Science proves that otherwise.

Once I had those two routines in place, I added another one of my favorites: my Sunday reset routine. I didn't start this one right away. It's a routine I wish I had known about and started much sooner. When the twins started kindergarten and we had four kids in school, with early mornings and busy afternoons, I knew it was time to implement this routine. It's become an anchor for our entire week. It takes about one to two hours, and it's the reason our weeks feel calm instead of chaotic.

I do it on Sundays, but honestly, you can choose any day that works for your family. It doesn't have to be Sunday—it's really just a reset routine. If you're a shift worker or have a shift-working spouse, and Sunday isn't your day off, then pick a different day. Maybe it's Wednesday. Choose whatever makes sense for your family dynamic.

As part of this routine, we get caught up on laundry (mainly the kids'), because by doing OLAD (one load a day), I'm usually pretty on top of it. This step is about making sure, before the week starts, that all the kids have their clothes set out and ready to go.

We use the 5-shelf weekly clothes organizer for kids, hanging closet storage unit for school outfits, and I make sure each child has their outfits picked out for the week, because I do not want to deal with clothing battles at 7 a.m. on a Monday. Trying to find a favorite shirt when you're already late? That's not a situation I'd wish on anyone. If you know, you know (IYKYK). You want to handle that stuff ahead of time—at a moment when you're calm, patient, and not rushed. So when I say I'm catching up on laundry, I'm really focusing on my kids.

Then I move on to food prep.

But before Sunday, I make sure my groceries for the week are delivered. Yes, you read that correctly. I switched to grocery delivery seven-plus years ago, and it was the best decision we have ever made for our busy family. Do you know that studies show the average American spends more than fifty-three hours each year grocery shopping at a local grocery store?[1] Plus, the average American reports spending more on impulse purchases. If you are still going into the grocery store every week, consider switching to having your groceries delivered.

If you hate cooking like I do, consider an online meal delivery service. Here's one thing I noticed: if I was feeling stressed and overwhelmed with making dinner, I would often cave to fast food or DoorDash. Look at your week; if you are eating out several times (whether breakfast, lunch, or dinner), look into a meal delivery service. We have found it to be more affordable than constantly eating out. Plus, you are able to eat healthier, have leftovers, and still sit down together as a family with a delicious home-cooked meal. Each week, I have two dinners delivered to me, mostly prepped. I usually only have to spend twenty-plus minutes getting the meal ready. This has been a huge win/win in our family. I've used a home delivery meal service for more than six years.

This also helps so much with decision paralysis. The constant thought and decision of *What are we going to eat this week?* can paralyze any busy and tired mom. Then you have to find the recipe and see if you have all of the ingredients. With a home delivery service, all of that is handled for you. What a stress relief!

Now, I just rotate through my top ten family favorite recipes and let my meal delivery service handle the creative side of trying new foods. Having a meal delivery service has been a game-changer for our family.

During my Sunday reset routine, I double-check which meals

---

1. Rebecca Lake, "Grocery Shopping Statistics: 23 Fun Size Facts to Know," *CreditDonkey*, July 2, 2020, creditdonkey.com/grocery-shopping-statistics.html.

are being delivered for the week, and prep food for the other dinners, plus sandwiches for the week. I'm not making four sandwiches every single morning, five days a week. Instead, I batch them all at once. We restock snacks. I also chop fruits and veggies to have lots of snack options ready to go for those busy after-school afternoons.

We glance at the calendar to see if there are any appointments coming up that we might have missed, just to go into the week prepared and aware of what's ahead.

We do a quick tidy of the main living areas to help our brains feel clear and calm as we step into another full week of mom life.

This routine is not fancy. It's not perfect. But it's effective: it works.

Every time I skip it, I feel the difference. And then I make sure not to skip it again the following week. When I'm consistent with it, I always thank myself by Tuesday. It's one of the best routines to have, especially if you're a busy family with lots of activities and moving parts.

What I've realized is this: the more routines I added, the less stress I felt, and the more emotional margin I had for my kids. Things felt easier. Tasks got done faster. And I started to notice I had hours of extra time back in my week, even though everything was still getting done.

These rhythms and routines weren't just about housework.

- They gave me back my capacity.
- They calmed my nervous system.
- They gave my family structure and predictability, without rigidity.

This is how routines evolved in our home, not as a punishment or a productivity obsession, but as a much-needed solution. It became a way to make space for the life we wanted to live.

Before routines, I loved planners. I was obsessed with planners, much like to-do lists. But once I added routines, I was able to ditch the planner. Planners are so pretty and they seem like the best idea ever, but in reality, they are just routines disguised. Because once you master routines, you don't need a planner to manage your daily tasks, even if they are pretty.

If you love planners, you might realize that *routines* are way more effective than planners. So often in motherhood, we are looking for that huge, big victory. Like if I can just add this one thing to my life, then everything will get easier. What daily effective routines showed me is that it's not about one big change; it's all about many small changes.

Routines are small, little changes that you bundle all up together to create a huge change: a morning routine, an evening routine, or a Sunday reset routine. When done consistently over time, those routines have huge results. And so I was starting to see huge results in these small daily changes that I was making by adding these effective routines.

Things were feeling easier. I wasn't stressed anymore, and it was starting to work. I stopped trying to master everything overnight and focused on just one small change each day. For me, that started with making my bed and waking up before my kids.

Nothing fancy. Nothing extreme. But even just doing one load of laundry a day has been game-changing for me.

These small changes built momentum. And once I had that down, I started stacking on other habits, adding a new routine one at a time, slowly but intentionally, until the days that used to feel chaotic started to feel easy and calm.

These routines gave me the confidence to keep going. I no longer needed to white-knuckle my way to a perfect system. I began to trust that small, daily changes would bring the results I was looking for.

I don't do it all. I just do a few small things really well, consistently, and they've made all the difference in the world.

A lot of moms who crave freedom and spontaneity think routines will trap them in a rigid schedule. But the truth is: routines are fluid. When built correctly, they actually create freedom. They add flow to your day because they're designed to serve you, not the other way around.

When your home is chaotic and messy, it begins to control you. It creates stress. You become a slave to your space, constantly reacting to the mess. It drains your time, your energy, and your mental clarity. But when you add routines, suddenly the home starts working for you. The burden lifts. Life feels easier.

And that perspective? It's game-changing.

If you're new to routines and just starting out, it may feel hard at first. This is not because routines are inherently hard, but because new things can feel hard.

So start slow. Add one thing at a time. Focus on consistency, not perfection.

It takes about twenty days to build a habit. If you want to exercise every day, aim to do it for twenty days straight. That's how you build the "habit-stacking muscle." I approached routines the same way.

I reminded myself: *I'm starting something new. It's going to feel weird and hard at first, because it's different.* So I gave myself time for it to feel easy before I added anything else.

At their core, routines are a practical form of habit stacking. Once you identify a routine and do it consistently, you've built a habit, and that's when it starts to run on autopilot.

Think of it like this: have you ever driven home on a route you've taken a million times, only to arrive in your garage and realize you don't even remember the last few turns? You didn't have to think, *Make a right here, now a left, now stop at the red light...* Your brain didn't need to consciously walk you through it because it had done it so many times before. You were on autopilot.

That's exactly what routines can do. Only you're not in a car— you're in your home. And that routine you mapped out? It becomes second nature.

But the opposite is also true. Have you driven to a new place? For me, I need the music off, I am hyper-focused, driving slowly, double-checking my maps. It feels difficult and unfamiliar. But I've driven a million times, so why does this still feel hard?

Because you're in a new place.

So start small. Make it feel easy. Have patience. Give yourself time. It will feel hard the first couple of times. Not because it is hard, but because it is new.

Here's how you start:

Pick your first routine; let's say it's a morning routine. Identify four or five things that you will add to your routine, then go and practice them every day until they feel easy. It probably won't take twenty days, but at some point, you will suddenly realize it feels easy and not hard anymore. You'll realize that you're doing your morning routine without any effort or real thinking involved; your body just knows to start doing it. That is autopilot.

It will free up so much mental capacity. Because if my brain doesn't have to focus on that constant: *Do the laundry now. Take the clothes from the washer. Put them in the dryer. I need to empty the dishwasher. Should I do it now? Or later?* Those thoughts take up a lot of space in our brain and are exhausting. But if my morning routine feels easy and autopilot, I will have more mental capacity to handle that toddler tantrum that is definitely going to happen later today.

So if you're reading this and you wait until the end of the week to tackle the mountain of laundry for your family, try doing just one load a day. Think about how overwhelming it is for your brain to look at a massive pile and think: *Now I have to sort, fold, and put all of this away.* By doing one load of laundry a day, you're still washing the same amount of clothes each week, but you're managing the mental load more effectively. It's much easier to do one small load every day than to spend three-plus hours doing seven loads on a Saturday.

Motivation isn't enough to keep up with everything as a busy mom. You need tools that support you both mentally and physically. So many moms say, "I can never get up before my kids. If I make any noise, they wake up," or "They already get up at 5:30 a.m.—I'm not waking up any earlier than I have to." And I get it. It's not for everyone. And it's not for every season of motherhood.

But I will say this: if it's something you can do, I 100 percent stand behind it as one of the best decisions I've ever made. There's something so life-changing and motivating about knowing that you at least started ahead, even if the rest of the day goes awry.

I introduced independent play early on with my kids, and if they woke up early, they would do that. There are tools for early risers. But just like anything, independent play takes time and patience to teach young toddlers and kids. Still, it's one of the best tools I've found for getting hours of kid-free time throughout the day.

I love using independent play during early wake-ups, transition times, in lieu of a nap (once they've outgrown it), or during dinner prep, so I can have peace and quiet while I cook. If you're completely new to routines and want to start, here are a few things you can do tomorrow:

- Make your bed
- Start one load of laundry
- Empty the clean dishes
- Reset common areas
- Run the robot vacuum
- Wipe down the toilets with a disinfectant wipe (if you have boys, you know this is needed daily!)
- Bonus: Go for a walk or move your body in some way

I promise you'll feel different, just like I did. It may become so addictive that you keep going and start adding other routines to your life and home.

Routines became the rescue I didn't know I needed. They brought structure where there was chaos and predictability where there was stress. They gave me the margin and breathing room I had been missing.

Motivation is great—when you have it. But routines show up even when you don't feel like it. Even when life is hard.

One of the things I love most about routines is how they ease the mental load. That term is finally getting the attention it deserves, more now than in any other decade of motherhood. Moms today are drowning in the invisible tasks that make up the mental load.

And that mental load? It's all those never-ending to-dos running through your head:

Don't forget to sign the permission slip. Pick up groceries. Fold the laundry. Schedule the appointment. Take the chicken out to thaw. It's relentless. It's exhausting. It eats up your brain energy.

Routines help manage that load. They simplify the laundry, the dishes, the errands, the groceries, and the meal planning.

So when moms come to me feeling overwhelmed and exhausted by the weight of it all, I *know* what they're experiencing —because I've been there. And I know what will help, because it helped me.

I walk them through how to add simple daily routines.

And the best part? Routines don't have to be fancy or complicated.

The simpler they are, the better. You need them just to work for you in the season of life that you're in, for your lifestyle, your personality, and your family dynamic.

YOUR TURN

Don't just read it—live it!

1. What routine are you going to add today?

_____

_____

_____

_____

_____

2. What tasks are you going to do during that routine?

_____

_____

_____

_____

Taking the step of creating your very first routine proves that you're really going for it! You're taking action and expecting results. Apply what you've learned and see the difference right away.

CHAPTER 4
REDEFINING PRODUCTIVITY FOR MOMS

The number of planners I've bought, started, and never used consistently is embarrassing. So much money was wasted chasing the hope of finally finding the perfect tool to manage my life and all its moving pieces.

Those beautiful leather-bound planners—with color-coded sections, a tab for every month, and even spots for gratitude, meal planning, goals, and hourly time blocks—promised the dream of organization. Just holding one made me feel like I was on top of the world. I was convinced that simply buying the planner would make all my organizational dreams come true.

But here's the thing: planners work best when you don't have unexpected events, constantly changing schedules, and thousands of daily interruptions. And that definitely doesn't describe life as a busy mom of four.

If you can write down a task and trust that it will get done, or assign a deadline and stick to it, then planners work. But they require dedicated, uninterrupted time to focus and complete what's written down.

As a mom, my reality looked more like baby blowouts, toddler meltdowns, or unexpected trips to the pediatrician. I didn't have 100 percent control over my time, and that's when I realized: a generic planner just wasn't going to cut it.

So I tried apps and phone notifications. But those quickly became background noise—just more alarms I'd hit snooze on. None of these tools seemed to work for a mom constantly running in ten different directions.

Then I discovered routines.

Routines helped me realize that I didn't need to check every box; I just needed to focus on the key things that kept our home running and my stress levels low.

Here's how I manage it now, with kids:

- I get a few home tasks done first thing as part of my morning routine.
- I use a daily reset routine to stay on track throughout the day.
- I wind down with an evening routine.
- I automate whatever I can: online subscriptions, grocery delivery, and automatic bill pay.
- I use a digital calendar app for appointments and errands.
- I rely on anchors to help trigger and sustain my routines.

I no longer need hundred-page planners or long, overwhelming to-do lists. It's simple, streamlined, and effective.

Now, I have the capacity and breathing room to stay calm with my kids. My brain feels clear. The mental load is lifted. No more brain fog or decision fatigue.

This means even when the day takes an unexpected turn, I have a plan that keeps the home running without falling behind or feeling overwhelmed.

Productivity as a mom isn't about maximizing output. It's about making space for constant interruptions, fostering connection, and prioritizing calm.

Here's a perfect example: Before I had daily routines, my planner always had *"Do laundry"* written on it. Laundry felt like my nemesis—always looming. Once I implemented routines and adopted the one load a day (OLAD) strategy, I added laundry to my morning routine. That one change meant I no longer had to remind myself seven times a week to do laundry. Removing that mental reminder freed up so much space in my mind.

Before I discovered OLAD, piles of laundry haunted me everywhere. It took over my entire weekend: mismatched socks, wrinkled shirts, stained toddler clothes piled high. I felt exhausted before I even started, overwhelmed just looking at it all.

I hated laundry. I'd try to turn laundry day into "me time" by putting on a show I loved, but I still never felt caught up. The piles were always there.

Then one day, I was frustrated with myself because I had forgotten to move the laundry from the washer to the dryer. By the time I remembered, I had to rewash it. That was the moment I knew: *this isn't working.*

Shortly after, I discovered the one-load-a-day method. And from that moment, I was hooked.

I decided to stop saving it all for one massive, stress-filled laundry day on the weekend and instead completed one load, start to finish, each day: wash, dry, fold, and put away. No more laundry marathons, no more piles staring at me, reminding me of what I hadn't done, and to my surprise, it worked. One load felt doable, even on the busiest days, and combining this strategy with effective routines made it even easier. I no longer had to try to remember to do laundry. It became part of my quiet rhythm in the background of our home, something I could accomplish without stress. The mental shift was huge.

The easiest way to start OLAD is to create a schedule. Look at your week and break down your laundry by category or by person. For example, I do all my husband's clothes in one load. My clothes go in another load. Each of my four kids has their own individual load. So one of the first things you can do is break your schedule down by person, then by type of clothing.

For instance:

- All towels go in one load
- All sports or baseball clothes get their own load
- Sheets and bedding get their own load

If you look at your week and say, "Okay, I have my husband, myself, kids, towels, sheets, and maybe one or two extra loads," you might only have five loads total, especially if you don't have kids yet or you live in a smaller household. Beyond the philosophy of doing one load a day, the key shift is separating laundry by person. Because if you really think about it, when you put clothes away, you put them away by person. And when you mix all the laundry together, most of your time is spent sorting.

You throw everyone's clothes into one washer, move them to the dryer, and then you have to sort everything just to return each item to its owner's room, closet, or drawer.

And let's be honest: no one stores their entire family's clothes in one drawer.

So how do you save time? You get in front of the sorting.

And how do you do that? You wash by person.

If you wash your own clothes as a single load, then when they're done, you just put *your* clothes away. No sorting. No extra folding, unless you want to. Just hang them or drop them into drawers. Honestly, I don't even fold. I just put the clothes in the drawers. No more separating socks, either. You know all the socks belong to the same person—just toss them in. Same for underwear. It's all yours—no sorting needed.

When each person's laundry is done separately, you eliminate the biggest time-suck and mental drain: sorting.

The second biggest source of laundry stress is decision fatigue: *What am I washing today? When should I do it?* That's where a schedule comes in.

For example, my schedule looks like this:

- Monday: My husband's clothes
- Tuesday: My clothes
- Wednesday: Towels
- Thursday: Sheets
- Friday: Miscellaneous/kids' sports
- Saturday–Sunday: My kids (two kids per day)

Now I don't have to think about it. The day decides what I'm washing.

The only remaining decision is *when* to do it. That's where a routine comes in.

If you build your life around routines, you'll find natural anchors to help you stay on track. For me, I start my laundry every morning. And my anchor, the thing that reminds me to start my load, is when I get dressed for the day. Each morning, when I change out of pajamas and into clothes, that's my cue to start the washer. Then, at night, when I return to my bedroom and pass the laundry room, that's my anchor to fold and put away the load that's in the dryer.

I use anchor routines and a schedule, and I wash each person's clothes every single day separately. This is how I manage the mental load of laundry, and why I don't ever have piles. And that's something I never have to think about. And it's on autopilot because it's through routines, anchors, and OLAD.

If your household is smaller, you will do fewer days of laundry.

ANCHORS

In order for your routine to become autopilot—meaning something you do automatically without thinking—it helps to have something that kickstarts the routine. This is known as an anchor.

> An anchor is anything you already do automatically in your day.

An anchor is anything you already do automatically in your day.

For instance, you wake up every day. You brush your teeth, go to the bathroom, and get dressed. Ideally, you eat three times a day and drink water. These are things you don't have to remind yourself to do—they're already on autopilot because they're basic hygiene or survival habits. So, you can tie your routines to these anchors.

The anchor tells your brain: *It's time to start this routine.* For example, if I want to build the habit of making my bed each morning, my anchor is simply getting out of bed. I train myself to make the bed immediately after getting up.

I don't wait. I don't tell myself I'll come back to it later, because as we all know, later rarely happens. And when you delay, you're adding to your mental load by putting "make the bed" on your internal mental to-do list. The goal is to stop adding tasks to your mental list and instead leverage anchors to help you take action with minimal effort.

Use the anchor to immediately push you into the routine:

- The anchor for making your bed is getting out of bed.
- The anchor for working out is putting on your workout clothes.
- The anchor for starting laundry is either walking past the laundry room or changing into clean clothes—both remind you to do that one load.
- The anchor for running your robot vacuum is placing it somewhere visible, so passing by it reminds you to start it.

I use anchors to help me remember to do errands. For example, my son has an appointment each week; it's in the calendar, and I know we have this mandatory appointment for him. I also want to wash and clean my car each week, because I am a mom and my car is a hot mess if I don't clean it weekly. My anchor for remembering to wash and clean my car is my son's weekly appointment. The appointment is already on the calendar, so I anchor my car getting cleaned with my son's appointment, and now I never forget to get my car cleaned. I treat this weekly errand as a routine, something I do every week without having to think about it.

I teach routines based on the foundation of anchors—every routine gets tied to one.

When you use anchors and routines together, they eliminate brain fog and the mental load that moms carry. You no longer have to ask yourself, *When am I going to get this done?*

You no longer need a mental checklist constantly running through your head: *I need to make my bed, start the laundry, do the dishes, drive the kids, get my car cleaned, prep dinner…* That list disappears because it now lives in your routines.

You're no longer weighed down by all the things you used to manage in your mind. You trust your routines. They carry the mental load.

All those lists we, as women, moms, and homemakers, used to carry around in our brains: they're gone. Your mind can finally feel clear and free because you've transitioned that responsibility to anchors and routines.

These laundry hacks have been a game-changer for me and my family. Because of these changes, all of my kids, even the seven-year-old, now do their own laundry. They start the washer, move clothes to the dryer, and put them away each week. Because the truth is, teamwork really is the dream work, and moms weren't meant to do it all alone.

I'm no longer buried under piles of laundry. I have systems and tools that actually work. A small, daily win I can count on. No more kids yelling at me for clean socks. No more frantic scrambling to see if the baseball uniform is washed before a game.

OLAD, routines, and anchors didn't just change my laundry—they changed my mindset.

It reminded me that I didn't need big, dramatic, huge overhauls and changes every day. I needed sustainable habits that could give me back my energy, sanity, and weekends. One load, one win every single day.

And I didn't stop there.

RESET ROUTINES

It all started with a timer.

Out of desperation, I bought a large, highly visible countdown timer. At the time, I was stuck in a cycle of constant nagging, repeating myself ten times, and getting nowhere. I felt like I was always yelling, always correcting, always cleaning, and no one was listening. But when I introduced the timer, everything changed. The visual cue gave my kids a sense of structure and urgency without me having to say a word.

Suddenly, transitions weren't full of whining, cleanup time didn't feel like a battle, and I could say, "Let's do a ten-minute reset," and have all hands on deck. They could see time passing. They knew the expectation.

That's when I started leaning into what I now call "reset routines." These are quick, structured windows throughout the day when we pause, clean, reset, and breathe.

A twenty-minute reset in our home looks like this: I announce it, we all come together and put our hands in like a sports team before a game, the kids pick fun, loud dance music, we start the big timer, and we all get to work. We make it fun, make it a game, and we celebrate with a reward afterwards. It doesn't have to be huge: sometimes it's a bike ride with mom, other times it's ice cream, and sometimes it's iPad or technology time. I'm a huge fan of motivating with incentives, making it quick, and making it fun.

Before starting the timer, I explain my expectations. Sometimes I assign tasks; sometimes the kids pick—but I reserve the right to veto or reassign if needed. It's playful, productive, short, and sweet.

And because this has worked so well with my kids, I started doing it for myself, too.

In the evenings, when I'm doing my "closing shift" and resetting the kitchen, I'll set the clock and race it. Turns out it's just as powerful for adults as it is for kids.

While I call it "race the clock," the actual name is the Pomodoro Technique. It's a science-based time management method that breaks work into twenty-five-minute intervals called pomodoros, separated by short breaks. Research has provided evidence that it helps "improve focus, reduce burnout, and increase productivity."[1] It was fascinating to learn that something I had been practicing for years is scientifically proven to be one of the most effective ways our brains work. I almost fell out of my seat when I found the website and realized, *This is why it works so well for me and my kids.*

So if you ever question whether it's effective, know that it's backed by science. And it's an amazing tool worth using and leveraging in your everyday life. This tool works incredibly well if you get easily distracted, start projects but don't finish them, or find yourself spinning in circles at home without making real progress. I would strongly recommend giving it a try.

We use other visual tools too. Over the years, depending on the kids' ages, we've used daily checklists with pictures for those who couldn't read. I've taped images to the kids' drawers so they know what clothes go where.

All of these tools empower my kids to be independent and work as a team in our home.

Because the truth is, tools help our brains relax. They create structure, predictability, and confidence. These tiny systems are what keep us from spiraling. They don't eliminate yelling completely—we're still human, living on grace, not perfection—but they do reduce the chaos. They lighten the mental load: that constant pressure of remembering everything and reminding everyone.

One of the biggest challenges in modern motherhood is exactly that: the mental load. We're inundated with constant data and decisions that can lead to overwhelm and decision paralysis.

---

1. Francesco Cirillo, *Pomodoro Technique Website*, 2025, https://www.pomodorotechnique.com/.

Systems save brain space. They mean you don't have to remember everything. Everyone shares in the responsibility of managing the home. They've made our home feel easier to manage because everyone knows what's expected—and those expectations are simple and visual. Stress goes down. Teamwork goes up. And the house feels just a little lighter every day.

Let's all *race the clock*. Rewriting the rules of getting things done. When you have amazing tools like *race the clock* in your back pocket, you look at messes differently.

My kids can make an in-home Rube Goldberg machine, using books, dominoes, construction paper, legos, and "home" stuff everywhere, and I can walk in, and instead of getting frustrated by the insane mess that was just made in minutes, I can join them in their world of creative play and know that we have tools to manage this mess later. Tools that will have the mess cleaned up in minutes versus hours. Tools that leverage teamwork and don't fall completely on me as "Mom."

I guarantee you will react less when you know it's not just you cleaning up the mess.

So as a mom, I now enjoy creative play, let loose, and don't stress. It's the perfect equation for becoming a more present mom and a less reactive one.

I love these tools so much because they give you the freedom to pause and let go of constantly feeling like you need to be busy in your home.

"Because you can literally sit while playing a game with your kids and look around your home and realize nothing needs your immediate attention."

That is the power of these tools. And so, you get to be present in the moment with your kids without the mental load weighing you down anymore, without the stress and the lies that we tell ourselves that we constantly need to be busy in our homes. You have confidence now in your home, where you can sit and be still and be present and enjoy quality time with your kids and let go of the constant need to feel busy.

You start to realize that present moments are the basis of perfect days. Once you're no longer spending your whole day feeling like you have to stay busy cleaning, and instead get to be present—playing games with your kids, laughing over Connect Four, building forts in the family room—those are the days you'll look back on and think: *That was worth it.*

Those are the perfect days of motherhood. I don't have to live in a constant state of stress and chaos anymore. I get to sit, enjoy, and be present in these priceless, ever-fleeting moments.

To the mom who feels guilty for not being present with her kids because the constant to-do list is always nagging at her: Yes, I felt that too in the beginning.

But what I realized is, the more I got my home on autopilot, the fewer things there actually were to do in the moment. The nagging stopped. And suddenly, being present felt easier—because there was finally space and time for that.

To the mom who's struggling: Give it time. Have patience and grace with yourself. You'll get there too. The more you focus on routines, tools, and creating a teamwork environment, the faster things get done—and the more time you'll reclaim.

Remember: Quality time with your kids is more important than how clean your home is. Don't get caught up in tying your identity to having a spotless house.

For me, reducing the stress caused by my home's chaos wasn't about appearances, it was about my mental health. I was tired of feeling overwhelmed and on edge. It was affecting me, my health, and how I showed up as a mom.

The same goes for why I prioritize moving my body and exercising every day. I don't do it for a six-pack or to lose weight. I do it for mental clarity and emotional balance. You need to move your body daily because it gives you the endorphins you need to show up with energy and joy to be an active, engaged, present mom. Whether it's working out or cleaning your home, the root purpose is the same: to create space and capacity so you can be the kind of mom you want to be.

And now, because I've stuck to my anchors and routines, everything gets done on time, with very little mental effort.

And that, truly, is a beautiful thing.

YOUR TURN

Don't just read it—live it!

1. Write out your weekly laundry schedule.

_____

_____

_____

_____

_____

2. What routine will you add OLAD to?

_____

_____

_____

_____

_____

3. What time of day makes the most sense to use *race the clock*?

_____

_____

_____

_____

_____

Taking the step of getting your laundry on autopilot and using *race the clock* to get more done in less time will free up so much of your time and mental energy. Apply what you've learned and notice the difference right away.

CHAPTER 5
CREATING A FUNCTIONAL HOME WITHOUT THE FANCY BINS

"Our outer worlds invariably affect our inner worlds and vice versa," according to Danielle Roeske, PsyD, vice president of residential services at Newport Healthcare.[1]

It was time my inward and outward spaces matched each other, and I wanted both of them to feel peace, calm, and clean.

WHEN THE PINTEREST HOME DIDN'T WORK

When I first started ditching the chaos in my home, I was obsessed with making my home look organized. The kind of setup that would get shared on Pinterest: the clear bins, the pretty labels, the matching baskets lined on a shelf. I spent money and time and way

---

1. Danielle Roeske, Psy.D., vice president of residential services at Newport Healthcare, quoted in *"The Mental Health Benefits of a Clean Home," Newport Healthcare*, January 26, 2023, https://www.newporthealthcare.com/resources/press/clean-home-benefits/.

too many late-night hours convincing myself these beautiful bins would eliminate the chaos. It felt good until I noticed it didn't work.

The truth hit after the twins were born.

I was recovering physically, sleep-deprived, and home by myself many days for ten-plus hours while my husband worked long days and commuted. I was desperate for any help I could get from my two older toddlers, who were just two and three years old at the time. But when I asked them to put something away or find something we needed, they were completely at a loss and couldn't help. I understood they were young, and I didn't get mad or frustrated, but it opened my eyes to a key missing element in our home.

I had focused so much on keeping our home organized, but it was far from functional.

I remember one day asking my three-and-a-half-year-old to do something simple: grab a pack of baby wipes from the twins' bedroom closet. I was feeding the twins in the family room and had run out of wipes, but I wasn't in a position to get up and get them myself. This kind of thing happened often.

Being home alone with four small kids, including newborn twins, there were countless moments when my hands were full and I couldn't perform even the simplest task. We had a nanny who helped and a very involved local family, but even with support, there were plenty of days when I was on my own, playing zone defense with four little ones. Not having the wipes where I needed them, when I needed them, was incredibly frustrating.

So I turned to my three-and-a-half-year-old (my oldest at the time) to help. After lots of effort and several attempts, he kept coming back empty-handed.

That's when it hit me: my home was not simple enough for my kids.

The systems I had built only worked if I was the one using and managing them. They were too complicated—not designed with a toddler in mind. My home was organized, but not functional.

I had set it up to look pretty, but no one else could help me with it. And being home alone with four young kids made me realize I no longer cared how it looked. If it wasn't helping me or serving me in my day-to-day, I didn't want it.

That moment of clarity was eye-opening and liberating. I was done organizing to meet someone else's standards. I was done arranging my home to look good in a photo—for Pinterest, for Instagram, for someone else's idea of "perfect."

So I let go of the idea that everything had to be pretty.

Instead, I started asking myself one simple question: "Can my kids do this on their own without me?" That became my new benchmark: not aesthetics, not perfection, but functionality.

> Instead, I started asking myself one simple question: "Can my kids do this on their own without me?" That became my new benchmark: not aesthetics, not perfection, but functionality.

I began creating systems even a toddler could use. And when I reimagined how our home functioned, one thing became very clear: If my kids couldn't use a system, it wasn't really a system at all.

Ask yourself this: *Do I ever have to stop what I'm doing to walk to another area of my home just to finish a task? Does my "organized" home actually work for me in real time?*

When we see a clean home, we often assume it's organized. But I'd argue otherwise.

I've been in many homes that looked organized—cute baskets, stylish labels—but when you opened them up, they were just filled with random clutter. They looked tidy on the outside but weren't functional on the inside.

Functionality means everything you need to manage your home is in the right place, at the right time, and is easy to access and use in the moment you need it.

Cleaning up becomes easier. Putting things away becomes faster. And anyone, even your two-year-old, can go grab an item in just a few steps, with very little effort. No more "I don't know where it is." No more "I can't do that." Just simple systems that work for everyone in your home, including the littlest ones.

How good does that sound? In short, if you ever have to stop a task and go to a different area of your home to finish or start what you set out to do, your home is not functional.

Here are some of the changes I made to make my home more functional:

- Baby wipes are stored throughout the home so messes and spills can be quickly cleaned: the hallway drawer, the kitchen, the laundry room, all bathrooms, and the car.
- A small broom, counter cleaner, and wipes are right next to the table or island for quick pickup after eating.
- Another one that I like is to store Clorox wipes (any kind of disinfectant wipe) behind the toilet in each of your bathrooms or under your sink to quickly clean the toilet and the sink.
- Labeled toy bins with photos instead of words. And make sure the baskets aren't stuffed, requiring expert Tetris skills to put the toys away. Instead, it should be easy-to-use containers with easy-to-snap-close lids, not stuffed, but with plenty of space.
- Their snacks went into a low, easy-to-reach drawer, and their clothes were folded onto clothes hangers instead of in drawers so they could access them on their own.

- Kids' plates and bowls are dishwasher- and microwave-safe and stored in a low, easy-to-reach drawer.
- I added Lazy Susans to my linen closet, medicine cabinets, refrigerator, and drawers so the items were easier to see and grab, not only for me, but for my kids and husband too.
- The dining room table has a clear plastic table cover so my kids can do art and school projects, and I don't have to worry or stress about stains or scratches on my nice table.
- I made everything as intuitive as possible because I wanted them to succeed without needing me to walk them through every step.

I learned this through my own trial and error. So many times, I was hunting through my house to find scissors when I needed them. So I put them everywhere.

I stopped being the bottleneck and started sharing the responsibility with others. For example, when my seven-year-old got a small cut on his hand, he didn't have to ask me where the Band-Aids were or if I could help him get them from a high cabinet because the Band-Aids were in a functional place, easy for everyone who lives in my home to access. A functional home means it's no longer just you. Your kids can be more independent.

I didn't want to have a home where I was constantly the bottleneck, where everyone had to come to me to solve their problems. I wanted a home where everyone could be their own problem solvers. And that's when I discovered having a functional home.

I now prioritize a functional home because I believe a lot of a mom's stress comes from feeling like she's the go-to for everything. It feels like everything falls on her shoulders. And a lot of times it does, because the home isn't functional enough for others to rise up, take the lead, and contribute. When a system is too confusing, too hard, or creates resistance, people are less likely to help. So naturally, they seek help, and you become that help, because you're the one who created the system in the first place.

I realized that organization helped me start this journey, but having a functional home is what got me to the finish line. You'll feel less stressed. It's a win/win.

When everything in your home has a home, putting things away instead of down is easier.

And the difference? Almost immediate. My kids started putting away toys without asking where they went. They began choosing their own snacks, getting dressed without help, and even resetting their play areas.

Using *race the clock* helped motivate even the toddlers who resisted teamwork.

We weren't perfect, but we were functioning better together. It reduced decision fatigue for everyone. Fewer questions. Fewer meltdowns. Less "Mom, where is this?" and more "I already did it." I shifted from being the manager of every task to the leader of a capable team. I stopped doing everything myself and started building a home where everyone knew how to pitch in. It felt easier.

Over the years, I've continued making small tweaks and changes. If I see my kids struggling with something, I'll ask them, "Does that feel hard?" Because often, kids aren't being lazy or disobedient, it just feels too hard. I've noticed that the easier and more functional our home has become, the less resistance, the more cooperation, and the greater independence my kids have developed. That correlation is not a coincidence.

I continue to view our home through my kids' eyes, making small changes where needed. As I always say (and as leadership expert Robin Sharma famously puts it), "Small changes, when done consistently over time, have huge results."

Before I simplified our home, weekends weren't restful. They were a chaotic race to catch up on everything that hadn't gotten done during the week. I would wake up Saturday already feeling behind. The kitchen needed cleaning. Laundry baskets were overflowing. Every surface seemed to scream for my attention. My to-do list ruled the weekend. Rest wasn't even on the radar.

I was constantly in motion but never felt caught up. Even when my body was tired, my mind couldn't relax. If I sat down for even a moment, guilt crept in. There was always something else to clean, prep, fold, or organize.

Then I started simplifying. Not just decluttering, but restructuring how our home functions.

I got serious about keeping only what we actually used and needed. I created systems for where things belonged, how we would reset certain spaces, and how we would share the responsibilities and the home load.

And slowly, everything changed.

Our home became easier to manage. Not because it was perfect, but because it was finally functional.

The emotional freedom that followed? It shocked me. I wasn't carrying the invisible weight of the house anymore. My mental load began to lift. I had breathing room. I could sit on the couch with my kids and actually relax, without guilt or overwhelm.

And it didn't just affect me. My relationship with my husband softened. I wasn't snapping out of stress or exhaustion anymore. I was more present. I laughed more. I had more space to see and enjoy the people in front of me, especially my kids. Simplifying our home gave me the breathing room I needed.

So stop and ask yourself: *How functional is your home right now?*

If you are in your bathroom, ready to clean and tidy, is everything you need in the space already? Or would you need to run to the garage for a broom, the laundry room for the toilet cleaner, and the kitchen for a washcloth?

We've all been taught to store things in the garage or the laundry room, and then we find ourselves running all over the house trying to locate what we need.

You can create a cleaning caddy, and many people do. But personally, I don't use one, because you still have to find a place to store it. And if it's not stored in the last place you need to clean, you end up hunting for it anyway. Instead, I prefer to store cleaning supplies exactly where you use them, so they're ready when you need them. Still, for some people, having a cleaning caddy to carry from room to room works just fine. At least in that case, all your supplies are in one place and accessible while you clean.

But here's the thing: we don't have a lot of time. And if your home is set up to be functional, with everything where you need it when you need it, then you can clean in short, thirty-second bursts. If you're using the bathroom and your kids are entertained for a moment, grab a Clorox wipe and quickly wipe down the toilet or counter. Use a baby wipe to clean the mirror. You can tidy the whole bathroom in under a minute, without ever leaving the room.

Because often, if you leave the room and pass by your kids, they'll see you and want your attention. That window of time, the thirty seconds or minute you had to clean, disappears. And that is the reality of motherhood. You have to take advantage of the moment you're given, and that's why I believe so strongly in making your home functional above all else. You need to be able to use every free second you're given, because it truly is a gift, and it's not guaranteed to come back.

Ask yourself this: *If I asked someone to grab something for me real quick, would they find it immediately? Or would they come back empty-handed, frustrated, and confused?*

Open your linen closet, your pantry, your medicine cabinet. If you asked your two-year-old to grab something from there, would they succeed?

> Ask yourself this: If I asked someone to grab something for me real quick, would they find it immediately? Or would they come back empty-handed, frustrated, and confused?

Creating an organized home with pretty baskets and matching containers did feel good. From the outside, everything looked neat. But it didn't solve my problem. It didn't give me the real solution I was looking for, especially when family members couldn't find anything. Even if I said, "Go to the closet. It's in the basket," it didn't help if the basket was just a pile of random stuff. If it was overstuffed or hard to see into, it wasn't truly functional.

That's when I thought of Lazy Susans. With a Lazy Susan, you can see everything. It prevents you from overstuffing, and it forces you to be intentional about what you keep.

You realize: I don't need four different types of lotion. Because at the end of the day, if I ask a family member to grab some lotion and there are too many options, they get confused and overwhelmed. They may know where the lotion is, but they don't know which one they're supposed to grab. That uncertainty can paralyze them.

So yes, having an organized home is great. But the goal isn't just for it to look good. It's to make it functional and intuitive for everyone, not just you.

It is in this sense that paring down and decluttering is a step toward creating a functional home. Because when there are too many options, people in your home will inevitably come back to you and ask:

- "Which one do you want me to use?"
- "Which one am I supposed to use?"
- "I don't know which one to use."

If your top priority is how things look—if you're focused only on making things pretty—you won't solve your real problems because the problems lie in the details.

You want people in your home to feel independent and capable. Your kids can do things on their own. We are often the bottlenecks to that independence. I constantly tell my kids, "I want you to solve your own problems. If there's something I can do to make that easier so you don't have to come ask me next time, let's fix that right now." I want them to come to me for the things they can't solve, not for simple questions like, "Where's the sunscreen?"

Sometimes, my kids ask for help with something I know they can handle on their own. I'll wait to respond (on purpose) and then hear, "Never mind! I figured it out myself." That's a win.

Don't be too quick to rescue your kids or solve their problems. Waiting a few minutes, or simply saying, "In a minute," gives them space to try on their own. That space is life-giving. It builds confidence and capability.

The other day, my daughter yelled from the kitchen, needing help with something. I was doing something else, so I said, "I'll be there in a minute." She didn't like how long I was taking (which was intentional), and then came running to me, beaming: "I figured it out! I did it all by myself!" If I had jumped up and rushed in to do the simple task for her, she would've missed that empowering moment.

But here's a big FYI if you're going to start empowering your kids more: You need to lower your expectations. Let me say that again: If you want your kids to feel capable, confident, and independent, you have to lower your expectations of what a "job well done" looks like, based on their age.

Have grace when accidents happen as they're learning, and always celebrate the wins, no matter how small they seem to you. To your kids, they are huge.

It won't be perfect, and that's okay! I must say this a thousand times: Progress over perfection. I'd rather have someone try and fail in my home than not try at all because they think they can't do it perfectly. Now, messing around and being careless when I know they're capable of more, that's another story. But what I'm talking about is genuine effort. If your child tries and fails, we clean up the mess together and try again.

I think one of the biggest lightbulb moments I've had, and that I've seen with many of the moms I coach, is realizing there's a difference between an organized home and a functional home. Most people don't even realize that distinction until I explain it. People talk about cleaning schedules, ruthless decluttering, organizing bins, and buying all the containers… but very few talk about making sure your home is set up to be functional.

And that's a huge missing piece, in my opinion. You just don't hear a lot of content around building a functional home.

Let's talk about small homes or limited cabinet space. The smaller your home, the less stuff you can have.

Is that fair? No.

Is it fun? No.

Is it reality? Yes.

But here's the thing with stuff: you can always add more stuff. If you get a bigger home, you can get more stuff, and you don't need a lot of stuff. So if you have a small house, you need less stuff.

Here's the first hard truth that a lot of people struggle with: Is it possible to have an easy-to-clean, autopilot home in a 700–800-square-foot space? Yes, it is.

Will you need less stuff? Absolutely.

Will you need to get very creative with your storage and cabinetry? Yes, without a doubt.

There are so many things you can store vertically or on the walls. You can use Command hooks, more wall shelving, etc. You'll need to think creatively about storage solutions.

Buy functional furniture: pieces that serve a purpose and offer extra storage. Ottomans, TV consoles, armoires, above-garage storage, under-bed storage containers on wheels, and hanging wall folders are just a few of the great options available today.

Yes, having more cabinets is helpful, but here's the other truth: If you have a larger home with a lot of cabinetry, you're more likely to buy and accumulate more stuff. And that still leads to chaos and overwhelm, because now you're managing more things. Even in a big home, I would still say get rid of the excess.

I have lots of cabinetry in my own home, but many of those cabinets are empty. Just because you've got the space doesn't mean you have to fill it. Because everything you bring into your home requires management. If you're not using it, you're still mentally managing it.

So I say: Let it go. Let your brain off the hook. Free up your time, space, and mental load.

Yes, with a small home and limited cabinetry, you'll need to get creative about storage. But having a functional home in a small space is just as important (if not more) because you need to be intentional about where things go and how they're used.

Before you buy something, ask yourself: *Do I know exactly where this will live?*

If you're at Target and see something you like, you should be able to clearly visualize where it's going to go in your home.

And if it's an item of clothing, you should know exactly which item you're going to let go of to make space for it.

I love the one-in, one-out method: for every item you bring in, you let go of one item.

It helps you manage the chaos and maintain balance as things come into the home. Because the more people you have in your household, the more stuff is coming in, and not nearly as much is going out.

Be intentional. Be clear. Because without boundaries, stuff piles up—and overwhelm follows close behind.

YOUR TURN

Don't just read it—live it!

1. What things in your home do you need to move or get rid of to make your home more functional?

_____

_____

_____

_____

2. Do you need more functional storage options?

_____

_____

_____

_____

3. Test it: Ask your kids to go and grab something, and see what happens.

_____

_____

_____

_____

Taking the step to create a functional (not just organized) home will free up so much time and mental energy and allow your kids to be more independent and capable. Apply what you've learned and see the difference right away.

CHAPTER 6
BUILDING TEAM PLAYERS IN YOUR HOME

Teamwork is light work that helps you go from a mom who does everything, feeling like Cinderella, to a family acting as a team who's in this together.

I remember this like it was yesterday. There was a season when I was doing it all: every load of laundry, every meal planned, every meal prepped, every area cleaned up, every toy picked up at bedtime. I was the default parent for everything, and it looked like I was holding it all together on the outside, but on the inside, I was hating it and growing resentful toward everyone.

I was constantly thinking, *Why am I the only one who sees the messes? If I don't do it, no one else will.*

I stopped aiming to do everything myself and started teaching my kids how to help in age-appropriate ways. I shared the weight of our home with my husband instead of carrying the unspoken mental load alone.

And you know what happened? Our house didn't fall apart. It came together. We became a team, and the relief that followed felt like oxygen. Teamwork didn't just lighten the load; it changed the culture of our home.

And I finally stopped feeling like I was drowning in the very life I prayed for, creating team players, not just participants. I was teaching my kids that they were not just passengers in our home but part of the team. This was probably one of the most impactful shifts we've made. It didn't happen overnight. It started small, especially since my kids were still under five years old at the time.

I introduced the idea of teamwork as light work, where everyone who lives in the home helps in the home. We started with one simple task: a morning routine. Getting dressed, making their bed, brushing their teeth, and putting their shoes in the bin by the door. And with age-appropriate knives, my kids learned to cut fruits and veggies or take their hamper from their room to the laundry room. These were small tasks, but they built a great foundation for more in the future.

I remember the first time, at four years old, one of my toddlers put all of her clothes away from her clean laundry basket, all on her own, using her weekly clothes hanger, with matching socks and underwear. It proved that they were capable and that I wasn't alone. And that, just maybe, this team thing was possible.

They needed reminders, lots of them, but I stayed consistent. I set up systems that made it easier: bins that were labeled, picture charts, a self-serve breakfast station, and snack stations so that they could complete tasks that matched their age and give them an early taste of contribution without it feeling like a consequence. And then the shift started to happen.

They began to take pride in it and would get so excited when they completed a task all on their own. Pride would light up their face with the biggest smile, especially if they started when they were young, because toddlers love to feel big and be helpful. So I played into those feelings and planted seeds with the intentional and strategic language that I used.

They didn't just help because they had to. They helped because it made a difference and allowed Mommy to be more available for fun moments too. Our home felt lighter, not just in the workload, but in the energy.

We have never been a mess-free home. We have four kids, after all. But now the messes get cleaned up faster, and I don't feel like I'm doing everything all by myself.

It gave them ownership, confidence, and a sense of belonging.

We were all a team, working together.

One of the hardest parts of shifting into a teamwork-driven home was the mindset. I see society telling women that they can do it all, work full-time, raise the children, be at all the important stuff, manage the home, and you don't need any help.

Not true. We need a village, not just outside of the home, but in the home too.

I've had many conversations with my husband and kids about how it's simply not feasible for one person to do it all. I explained the concept of the mental load, how it matters deeply, and how no matter how hard I try, I can't carry it all alone. Expecting myself to bear the entire burden isn't a strength; it's unsustainable.

So, I shifted my mindset. I started thinking like a coach, not a victim.

My job isn't to do everything. My job is to lead, to teach, and to guide. That means asking for help—kindly and without resentment.

Here are two real scripts I often use in our home:

- "Hey, come work with me in the kitchen to prep the fruit and veggies for dinner tonight. Everyone in our home is a team player, and this is how you can be part of the team."
- "I need you to get your laundry done today. It helps our family run smoothly and is your responsibility."

I've learned that when I frame a task as a statement of contribution, not as a question about compliance, my family is more likely to lean in. When you ask a question, there's room to say no. But when you set an expectation with a clear and respectful tone, it creates a different energy. Not always joyful, not always without a sigh, but more often than not, it works.

Of course, there are still groans, slouched shoulders, and the occasional sigh from the kids. I used to take it personally. But instead of snapping or shutting down, I learned to pause, breathe, and reframe.

I might say, "I get that this isn't your favorite thing. It's not mine either. But we're a team. Let's *race the clock* and knock it out fast so we can move on and do something fun together."

And I love to follow up teamwork with fun. When I barked out orders while everyone was tired and hungry, it didn't go well. But when I picked the right moment, gave a heads-up instead of a command, made it fun, and followed with something enjoyable, I got more cooperation every time.

Each time I stayed calm instead of snapping, I reminded myself: *I'm not just managing tasks, I'm teaching life skills. I'm building a home where everyone contributes and plays a role.*

It's my job, as their mom, to coach, not to be Cinderella.

A clean home used to feel like a fleeting miracle, something I might barely manage during nap time or after bedtime, only to see it unravel within an hour of the kids waking up. I'd clean one room while they destroyed another, chasing chaos in circles. That changed when we introduced family resets.

A reset is a short, intentional block of time where everyone stops what they're doing and helps bring the house back to baseline. We don't aim for perfection, just functional and guest-ready.

If we're home all day, doing life together, we'll do several resets throughout the day and week.

- **Morning Reset:** Everyone makes their bed, puts misplaced items back in their room, and does a five-minute tidy of common areas.
- **Afternoon Reset:** Just before screen time or going outside, we clean up from the first half of the day, dishes, lunch mess, and toys.
- **Evening Reset:** After dinner but before bedtime, we all pitch in to tidy the kitchen, living room, and shared spaces.
- **Sunday Reset:** My favorite! We spend dedicated time preparing for a smooth, successful, stress-free week. Each child has age-appropriate tasks. My youngest might unload plastic dishes or put shoes in a basket. My oldest might gather trash and take the bins to the curb.

It's not about equal contributions. It's about everyone participating, recognizing their strengths and limitations, and working together.

Here's what I learned the hard way: resets only work when tasks are clear, simple, and predictable. When I tried to wing it, the kids got overwhelmed. When I micromanaged, they got frustrated and gave up. But when I used checklists, visual timers, and clearly defined roles, the pushback dropped and follow-through increased.

There were days I had to remind them repeatedly. Days I did more than my share just to get it done. But I was in this for the long haul. And I knew that with daily practice, it would eventually pay off.

Now, after years of consistent resets, we can tidy our entire living area in under fifteen minutes.

The results have been profound. I stopped cleaning alone at night after everyone went to bed. The house stayed livable; maybe not spotless, but guest-ready for longer stretches. The kids started noticing messes and taking initiative to clean them up. Our home no longer felt like a burden. It started feeling like a shared responsibility.

These twenty-minute resets may seem small, but they've saved us hours of frustration, endless mess, and constant chaos.

And they serve as a daily reminder: This isn't just my home to manage. It's our home to care for, together.

Yeah, I love resets! They are a huge mom hack. I have lots of videos on social media about all of us doing resets together.

My kids are very capable now. They kind of just know the drill. I have one reel I shared on Instagram. I set the timer for thirty minutes because our house was such a disaster. I think it was after Easter. And I thought it was going to take so long for all of us to do it together. We did it in twelve minutes. It was insane how quickly it went.

But we didn't start there. Like learning to ride a bike, we were clumsy and kept falling off when we first started. But once you get in a rhythm and you all know your zones and roles, you all work hard together.

We do a reward after every family reset. I always offer something afterward. Sometimes it's a small piece of candy, sometimes it's ice cream or a TV show. Many times, it's something we all do together, like playing a game or going on a quick bike ride.

The key to a successful family reset is this: Make it fun. Make it quick. And offer a reward afterward.

Want your kids to be team players, but not sure how to start the conversation? Try this: Use a sports team or farm analogy. Keep it simple, because you're explaining it to children. Your husband should ideally be part of the conversation too, but if he's not, it's not the end of the world.

I often get asked, "How do you get your husband on board if he's resistant to helping around the house?" So I'll answer both parts here.

If your husband isn't on board yet, start with your kids. In my experience, husbands often follow once they see their kids participating. I don't know what it is, but something about seeing their children pitching in seems to spark that shift. My husband is very much a team player now. But in the beginning, I started with the kids.

I explained the concept of the mental load to my husband, but things really started to click when I began doing resets with the kids—and he saw the impact. Now we all do resets together as a team, including him.

When talking to kids, I use simple analogies, like a basketball team or a farm: "If you had a basketball team and everyone on the team decided to sit down and stop playing, except one person, what would happen?"

Ask your kids:

- Would that team win the game?
- How would that one player feel?
- Would they feel resentful, angry, tired, overworked, frustrated?

Then explain: "That's what our family unit is like. It's not a one-person show. We're all living in this home, and our home is like the basketball team. Everyone here is a player on that team. If Mom is the only one 'playing the game' (cleaning, organizing, managing) how do you think she feels? Like a real team, we need everyone to do their part to win. Mom can't carry the whole game on her own."

Or, use the farm analogy: "If we had a farm, everyone (including the kids) would need to feed the animals and take care of them. It doesn't work if just one person does it. The whole family runs the farm together."

That's the concept. And I use it with both my kids and my husband. With your husband, you can go into more detail about the mental load. With kids, I keep it visual and relatable. For example, I'll say: "Let's say you want to have a birthday party. You come to Mom and say, 'I want a birthday party this year.'" From there, I explain what goes into that: the planning, shopping, prepping, inviting, decorating, baking, and cleaning. It gives them a glimpse into the invisible work behind the scenes, and it helps them appreciate and understand the bigger picture.

Your child making the request is just thinking about having a birthday party. But we, as moms and parents, know all of the hidden, unspoken tasks that go into planning that party: making the guest list, sending invitations, choosing the event type, location, and time, ordering or baking the cake, buying supplies, decorating, prepping, and cleaning up—it's a lot. That's why it's important to bring your kids into the conversation about the mental load. Instead of keeping it all unspoken, help them understand: "When you ask for a birthday party, you're not just asking for one event. Here's everything involved in making that happen."

The same thing applies to husbands. They often don't realize everything that goes into managing a household or raising kids.

They might say, "Let's sign so-and-so up for basketball,"—but they haven't considered:

- What league?
- What's the schedule?
- Do we need new clothes or equipment?
- How will they get there and back?
- Who's managing the sign-ups and communication?

I often coach moms to get loud about the mental load. Call out the unspoken tasks associated with every request, because if others can't see it, they can't understand it. And when people understand the full picture, they're more likely to empathize, contribute, and work as a team.

Don't assume they just know.

For decades, society has told us the home is our responsibility as women. And while I do see a shift starting to happen, it's still not the norm. I'm tired of the '50s mentality, where women are expected to carry the entire home on their backs. We need to stop sitting in our stress, just complaining. We need to take action to change the situation.

We're done playing the martyr. We're done gathering with our mom friends to vent about how hard and unfair it is, without doing anything to fix it.

To be honest, this is one of the least attractive patterns I see in motherhood spaces. There are so many tools out there to help you create a teamwork environment at home, so it doesn't all need to fall on you. You can explain the mental load to your family in a way they'll understand. You can work together.

Nothing changes if you change nothing. No one's coming to save you. Change things yourself. Empower your family to take ownership and responsibility in the home.

One of the biggest misconceptions I hear about teamwork is that kids aren't "old enough" to help or are incapable. But here's the truth: Kids are way more capable than most parents give them credit for.

Another misconception is that "it's faster if I just do it myself." And sure, it might be faster in the short term. But if you always do it yourself, your kids won't learn, and you'll stay stuck doing it all. Yes, it takes time and patience in the beginning. I won't lie about that. That's why I encourage moms to start early, while time is on their side. No child will be perfect when they're first learning. It's going to take time for them to feel confident and efficient. But it will happen.

I've been building our family's teamwork systems for several years now, and just recently, things really started to click. Now, our family resets take under fifteen minutes. We can go from a chaotic home to a clean one in minutes. And that's because I've been working with my kids since my oldest was two years old, giving them the time and patience needed to get better at their skills.

At first, it will feel like more work and effort than it's worth. Many parents give up too quickly because they don't have the time or patience to see it through. But this is a long game, and that's exactly why a lot of parents don't have their kids helping at home. They're looking at it from a short-sighted perspective.

Unfortunately, by the time kids are old enough to have the skill set to complete tasks quickly and efficiently, the teamwork mindset and lightwork culture may already be lost. Now they're preteens or teenagers. They have the ability, but not the attitude. They don't care, and you're met with resistance or apathy.

But if you start when they're younger, when they have the attitude and enthusiasm to help, you're working with kids who want to be involved. Sure, they might not have the ability yet. But that comes with time.

Have the patience to build the ability. Know it's a marathon, not a sprint. In the long run, it pays off.

YOUR TURN

Don't just read it—live it!

1. What three tasks/chores could your child(ren) start owning and being a team player in now?

_____

_____

_____

_____

2. Pick a day and time to sit down with your kids and husband and explain to them that teamwork is light work and that everyone needs to be a team player.

_____

_____

_____

_____

_____

3. Test it: When are you going to do your first family reset? What tasks will each person get?

_____

_____

_____

_____

_____

Taking the step to create a "teamwork is light work" home has huge benefits, including for you to stop feeling like Cinderella. Apply what you've learned and see the difference right away.

CHAPTER 7
INDEPENDENT PLAY AND SMOOTHER MORNINGS

HOW INDEPENDENT PLAY CHANGED EVERYTHING

Do you feel like you're your kid's activity director every day, trying to keep them entertained and busy so you can just for one second attempt to fold a load of laundry?

I've been there. There was a time when I couldn't go to the bathroom alone, much less make a phone call or drink a cup of hot coffee. My days were a constant stream of "Mom!":

- "Watch this, Mom."
- "I'm hungry, Mom."
- "Mom, play with me."
- "Mom, I'm bored! I have nothing to do."

While I love my kids deeply, I was running on empty, and the twins weren't born yet. The mental load of having to be "on" every second of the day was exhausting and unsustainable.

I discovered a different way: a way that allows your kids to play without depending on you. I was committed to seeing this through.

Independent play is a type of play where children are given the opportunity to explore and engage in activities on their own, without adult guidance or interference. You set your baby (once they can sit unassisted), toddler, or child up in a designated area, such as a crib, pack 'n play, a blanket on the floor, or their room, and they play independently with specific toys for a set period of time. The child remains in the designated area until the timer goes off, playing with approved STEM toys or activities.

Independent play is different from when a child spontaneously chooses to play on their own. Often, young toddlers will wander off and start playing by themselves, which is wonderful—but it usually doesn't last long before they come back looking for you. When you teach independent play in a structured environment, it becomes a different experience than solo free play. It's a controlled period of time, set by you, and it can last much longer than spontaneous free play.

HOW I INTRODUCED INDEPENDENT PLAY

I set up a bin of STEM toys on a blanket in the corner of the living room, where they couldn't see me but knew I was nearby. I used a large visual timer set for ten minutes and told my two-year-old, "This is your play spot while I do the dishes."

The first few times didn't go perfectly. My toddler came to find me, had questions, said he was thirsty, and I had to redirect him back to his blanket and gently reinforce the idea of independent play. But after staying consistent for several days, it started to click—and he did it!

That moment changed everything.

I started with ten minutes, then gradually increased to twenty minutes. I rotated the toys each time to keep things interesting—puzzles one day, magnet tiles the next, then sticker books. I avoided screens, batteries, or toys that required constant involvement. I made it part of our morning routine after breakfast.

It became our independent play time. No big production, just consistent boundaries. And something incredible happened: my kids got better at it.

This type of play helps children develop their social, emotional, physical, and cognitive skills. It nurtures problem-solving, creativity, independent thinking, and decision-making. Children learn to trust themselves, build self-confidence, boost their creativity, improve concentration, and strengthen their fine motor skills. Independent play teaches them that they don't need to be "fed" entertainment; they can enjoy themselves with their own interests and imagination.

It's important to clarify that independent play and solo free play are not the same. Independent play is a skill that must be taught. It doesn't typically emerge on its own. In contrast, solo free play is more instinctive; it's part of a child being a child. Independent play is built through consistency, practice, and patience. Over time, kids develop the "muscle" of playing independently, without adult interaction or constant engagement. They learn to explore their toys, engage their imagination, and create their own fun, all on their own.

In the following, I'll first talk about independent play, and then I'll address solo play. I'm discussing both because, as a busy mom, whether you're a stay-at-home mom or a full-time working mom, you want to have intentional, present time with your kids. But there's also that dream of your kids playing independently while you're at home getting things done, and they're not constantly needing you. That's the dream of motherhood. And these types of play can make that dream more realistic.

Independent play creates that space. And if your child transitions into solo free play afterward because you have set up stations around your home where they can explore freely, you are extending their independent time even further.

So let's say you get two hours of structured independent play. Then your child comes to find you, but naturally transitions into solo play, where they continue playing on their own while you're nearby. You've now extended your focused time from two to three hours, all without the child needing direct engagement from you. That's why I use both types of play in my home. It allows for more uninterrupted time and encourages my kids to build skills and creativity on their own.

As discussed previously, independent play is a structured type of play where children are set up in a specific area (like a crib, pack and play, blanket, or their room) with selected toys for a set amount of time. During this time, they play without adult guidance or interference. The space, toys, and duration are all decided by the parent.

In contrast, solo free play is more spontaneous and child-led. The child chooses where they want to play, which toys they want to use, and how long they want to play. There's no set structure; it simply happens when the child feels inclined to play on their own.

Independent play offers more structure and control. The child remains in the designated area until the time is up, playing with approved STEM toys or quiet-time activities that you've selected.

Does this sound too good to be true? Are you worried your toddler won't sit still or engage with just a few toys without your interaction? Don't worry. You might be skeptical, but your child can and will do this. And when they do, it will amaze you, delight you, and feel like one of the best things you've ever implemented.

Independent play promotes healthy development as your child grows. It provides a low-stimulation environment, introduces structure, and cultivates a skill that can serve them well into adolescence. It's good for children to learn how to play within a specific space, with limited freedoms. This kind of structure mimics the routines they'll experience in school, so teaching it early is a gift. Believe it or not, kids like boundaries. They may test them, but ultimately, boundaries provide the security and predictability they crave.

I first heard about independent play when I had just welcomed my second newborn. My oldest was barely two years old at the time. I hadn't been a mom for very long, but when I heard about this concept, I immediately knew it was something I wanted to try. I already sensed I couldn't give my oldest the constant attention he was used to, and that he was still seeking.

Independent play felt like the solution. Of course, it's a great practice even if you have just one child. But when you have multiple children, the ability to give each of them constant attention becomes less and less feasible. This approach gave me a way to meet both their needs and mine.

And then, once I had the twins, I was just overwhelmed with gratitude that I had learned all these things beforehand. I had my home on autopilot. I had already mastered independent play with both of my older kids. I'd figured out a lot of my mom hacks before the twins arrived, which I truly believe was God's blessing in my life. It was like God saying, *"Hey, I know what's coming for you."*

Now that my kids are older, I'm even more able to see the long-term benefits. My kids are incredibly creative. They'll say things like, "Hey, let's make airplanes!" or "Let's build a fort!" The other day I saw it firsthand. We only watch a limited amount of television in the mornings. It was a Saturday, and they had already had about thirty minutes of screen time. (This is also why I love pairing independent play with TV: it can be a reward and another way to extend their time without needing you to entertain them.) We had turned the TV off, and I told them, "Go outside and play or figure out something to do," because I needed to get some work done.

At ages seven, nine, and eleven, they came up with an egg drop competition. They spent two full hours designing their contraptions and figuring out how to protect their eggs so they wouldn't break on impact.

And I just thought: *That is such a great example.* I didn't feed them entertainment or give them an idea. They came up with it on their own. And they felt confident enough to follow through with it because they're used to being creative. I truly believe that's a testament to independent play and how I introduced it early.

By the age of three, all four of my kids were able to sit and engage in independent play for two hours. Research shows that this aligns with developmental milestones. It wasn't just a personal win. It was developmentally appropriate.

Of course, before age three, expecting two hours of independent play isn't realistic. That's why you start small and work your way up. If you begin around nine months or one year, once they're sitting up, they won't be able to go two hours. It's not developmentally feasible. But by the time they're three, they can, as long as you've built that consistent habit and stretched that "muscle" over time.

Because that's what it is: a skill. A muscle they're learning to use both in their brain and their body. And when they're developmentally ready to play for longer periods, they already have the muscle and the skill to do it.

That's when their creativity truly blossoms. They become incredibly independent, wonderfully imaginative, and fully capable of entertaining themselves. And it's not something they see as a punishment; they actually look forward to it. It's a positive time for them. A chance to decompress.

> Because that's what it is: a skill. A muscle they're learning to use both in their brain and their body. And when they're developmentally ready to play for longer periods, they already have the muscle and the skill to do it.

If a child is overstimulated, which is totally normal in a busy home, independent play can be so beneficial. It gives their body and nervous system a break. It helps them regulate. It's a form of self-regulation, just like how we, as adults, can get overstimulated by noise or sensory input. Absolutely, kids feel that too. And independent play helps calm their bodies and bring things back into balance when they're in that overstimulated state.

They started making up their own games. They learned patience, creativity, and problem-solving, all without me hovering over them. And for me, what started at ten minutes eventually got to two hours of kid-free time to do whatever I wanted or needed. I could breathe, think, show up, calm down, shower, and be a more present mom afterward. Even my mornings began to shift.

Instead of frantic chaos, we had rhythms. My son would get dressed and do independent play while I finished my morning routine, and then we would head into breakfast together. Independent play wasn't just a parenting tool. It became a lifeline for me. It was game-changing for me. And it reminded me that I wasn't just allowed to take space, but I needed to, for their sake and mine.

This is precious time I wish every mom had.

CREATING AN ENVIRONMENT THAT SUPPORTS INDEPENDENT PLAY AND FREE PLAY

The best days are when you can incorporate both independent play and free play. Kids naturally want to be busy and active, but it's not the parents' job to constantly feed them entertainment. Doing so actually sets them up for long-term frustration and dependency. The ideal approach is to use both types of play strategically throughout the day.

But I came to realize that neither independent play nor solo free play just happens. You have to intentionally design your home environment to support it. When I looked around our space, I saw too many toys. It was overwhelming and overstimulating for everyone.

After some quick research, I learned that kids actually play better and longer when they have fewer toy choices. Most of our toys were tossed into deep, tall baskets or buried under clutter in overstuffed closets. It looked organized, but it wasn't functional for encouraging focused, sustained play. My kids would pull out overflowing baskets and dump them on the floor just to find one specific toy.

No wonder we were constantly stepping on toys and feeling stressed by all the clutter.

So I started making changes. I reduced the number of toys, organized them into smaller, more manageable groups, and started rotating baskets weekly. No expert Tetris skills required, just thoughtful simplification.

I rotated the toys every couple of weeks to keep things fresh but not overwhelming. I got rid of anything that required a million pieces or needed my involvement to work.

Our favorites: magnet tiles and building blocks, pretend play items like play food, doctor kits, and toy kitchen gear, simple puzzles, and drawing supplies, all open-ended and quiet (unless they made the noise).

I also got smarter with placement. If I were making dinner, I would keep a basket of magnet tiles nearby. If I needed to do laundry, I had a simple basket with a few toys ready in the family room. This setup encouraged longer stretches of independent play. At first, I had to redirect a lot, stay consistent, and praise even five minutes of focused play.

I had to learn not to jump in every time they asked a question or tried to engage me. I had to resist asking what they were making or drawing. The hardest part? Staying silent and avoiding eye contact. But over time, things shifted.

They started to expect those moments of independent play, and their bodies began to need them. They built stamina. I built trust in the process. Eventually, independent play became a rhythm they truly loved.

That small shift in our environment created massive freedom. It empowered my kids and gave me the chance to actually get things done, or just rest without guilt.

And that's the key. I didn't feel guilty because I understood the benefits. I knew how good this was for their brain and emotional development.

> That small shift in our environment created massive freedom. It empowered my kids and gave me the chance to actually get things done, or just rest without guilt.

It wasn't only good for them; it was good for me, too. As it turns out, giving my kids the tools to thrive on their own was one of the most life-giving decisions I've ever made for our entire family.

We continued with this routine and rhythm for years. Then I blinked.

The twins were starting kindergarten. All four kids are in school. A huge milestone. But what came with it was chaotic school mornings.

SMOOTHER SCHOOL MORNING

All of a sudden my morning routine felt different. Entered a new kind of chaos. Getting all four ready in the mornings felt like something out of a disaster movie: scrambling to find shoes, kids melting down over the wrong shirts, me barking orders while mentally juggling a hundred tasks before 8 a.m.

Now we felt behind. flustered. starting the day in stress mode.

I remember one morning in particular: one twin refused to wear a shirt, the other spilled a full glass of milk, and my older two were arguing over socks. I hadn't brushed my teeth, let alone eaten.

And as we finally made it out the door, I sat in our driveway, turned around, and looked at my kids and said, "We will not be having our mornings feel like and look like this for the next twelve years. Tomorrow, things are going to look different."

Our mornings were setting the tone for the rest of the day. And if we didn't change how we started, everything else would remain difficult. So I began experimenting with small single shifts.

The first one: having my kids pick out all of their clothes on Sunday in our reset routine, using clothes hangers. The second: a visual chart for my kids that showed their morning steps to get dressed, eat, brush their teeth, and get their shoes on, so I didn't have to nag them. And last, I added a self-serve breakfast station, teaching my kids that they can be independent in the morning and help get their breakfast.

Nothing fancy, just grab-and-go options like fruit, yogurt pouches, pancakes, or muffins ready to go. It made them feel independent and gave me the extra five minutes I needed. I also had them use the condiment squeeze bottles for the milk so they could pour their milk and have cereal without making any messes.

Lastly, I continued to encourage independent play. It's a skill that, once learned, lasts a lifetime. For my early risers, I had them transition to independent play in the morning so they wouldn't wake their siblings or interrupt my morning routine.

Within a week, the energy in our morning shifted. Our mornings felt calmer, more predictable. We weren't yelling or rushing out the door or forgetting backpacks and shoes. Now, I will say kids will be kids, and we still have mornings that are rough sometimes, but they are not that consistent anymore. I could stop micromanaging my kids, and my kids could step up and be more responsible. They responded better than I expected with a routine they could follow. They didn't feel like I was always telling them what to do. They knew what to do, and it made them feel capable.

Rethinking our mornings wasn't just about being on time. It was about reclaiming our peace. The power of owning your mornings, how you start your day, impacts the rest of your day.

These days, a win in my morning is having my kids move through the morning routine with minimal reminders. It means I'm present and available but not micromanaging or getting frustrated.

This is always a bit controversial every time I mention it. One of the hardest (but most rewarding) changes I've made as a mom was waking up before my kids. It allows me to start the day with intention, prioritize myself, and calm my mind before I'm immediately pulled into responding to everyone else's needs.

I wake up in peace, not to loud screaming. I get to drink my coffee while it's still hot and check off a few household chores before the kids are even up. With multiple kids, including twins and some early risers, I've built a rhythm that's actually realistic.

My kids know what their morning looks like. If they wake up early, they know it's time for independent play until their wake-up clock goes off. They check their chore chart, grab an easy breakfast from the self-serve breakfast station, and start getting ready. I'm nearby to guide if needed, but I'm not directing every move. Some mornings are louder, messier, or more rushed, but we have a baseline, and that gives us room to flex when life happens.

Owning our mornings hasn't just helped logistically; it's given me mental and emotional margin. When the day starts with calm instead of chaos, I'm more patient, more present, and I'm not already behind before the day has even begun. That shift impacts everything, from the tone I use with my kids to how I tackle work, home, and motherhood as a whole.

Sure, my kids still wake up having those kinds of days. But I can handle it with a better attitude because I've already taken care of myself first.

Let's be honest: toddlers can be incredibly picky about clothes. You might find yourself in a full-blown battle at 7 a.m. over a shirt they suddenly hate. That's a true story for me, and I'm sure it is for many moms. So here's what works: If you're a working parent trying to get out the door on time, or just someone who doesn't want to start the day with a meltdown, designate a time at the beginning of the week (not in the morning!) to pick out clothes with your child. Let them be involved. It supports their independence and gives them a sense of control.

Another game-changer? The self-serve breakfast station. Honestly, I think it's one of my top mom hacks. If you provide age-appropriate foods that your kids can get on their own, it frees up so much of your time. You can still be present in the kitchen, but they get to feel independent, confident, and capable. That's something really valuable to start at a young age.

And then there's the chore chart. You can introduce one as early as age two. Just make sure to use pictures instead of words for little ones.

I recommend doing it in this order: first, set out the week's clothes; then prep the breakfast station; and finally, use the chore chart to help them stay on track.

The chore chart keeps the morning flowing and eliminates constant reminders. Instead of repeating, "Did you brush your teeth? Did you put your shoes on? Did you pick up your clothes? Did you… did you…" you can simply say, "Hey, have you checked your chart?"

It shifts the responsibility to them in a really empowering way. It encourages self-management and reduces the mental load on you.

YOUR TURN

Don't just read it—live it!

1. Do you have the correct toys to start Independent Play today?

_____

_____

_____

_____

_____

2. What time of day would make the most sense for your schedule to introduce Independent Play?

_____

_____

_____

_____

_____

3. Do you have a Kid Checklist you can start using?

_____

_____

_____

_____

_____

4. What foods could you prep ahead of time for a Self-Serve Breakfast Station?

_____

_____

_____

_____

_____

Taking the step to create Independence in your kids takes time, but it is so worth it. Apply what you've learned and see the difference right away.

CHAPTER 8
FINDING MY IDENTITY AGAIN

I wasn't trying to lose myself; I just got swept up in the demands of life with four little ones. With four kids, twins, diapers, naps, schedules, meal prep, laundry, dishes, school drop-offs, pickups, tantrums, bottles, and barely any sleep, my days blurred together in a cycle of caring, cleaning, and managing meltdowns. I loved my children, but the version of me I had once known was fading fast, and resentment was growing quickly. Before the twins, I had a career and an identity; I used my brain, solved problems, and 2020 was supposed to be my year, the year the twins would go to preschool, and I would pursue my career again.

After three years of being a full-time stay-at-home mom, I was eager to figure out what my next chapter would be to find myself again. Then came COVID. The world shut down, and my world got even smaller.

My dream and hope of pursuing a career outside of being a stay-at-home mom were put back on the back burner. No church gatherings, no mom groups, no family playdates. School was remote, with a kindergartener and a first grader, while also trying to keep two preschoolers entertained, safe, and quiet.

I was juggling Chromebooks, baby wipes, snack times, and spelling lists while trying to hold in my tears, anger, and resentment.

My thoughts began to shift: *I don't want to be a full-time stay-at-home mom anymore. I love my family, but I'm not using all my gifts and talents. I want more.* That thought hit hard. I felt guilty for even thinking about it, but I also knew it was true. Motherhood had filled my heart, and at the same time, drained my identity.

I had watched and supported my husband's career while losing mine in the process. Serving everyone else while ignoring and pushing my own dreams to the back burner. But sitting at home with four kids amid a worldwide pandemic made me realize I was worth fighting for, and I wanted more.

I want motherhood and...

That moment was the beginning of a slow, intentional journey back to myself.

In our home, we had built a dynamic that worked with having four young kids, a mom at home managing everything, and a husband working out of the home full-time, providing for us as the breadwinner. And while many might find this home life to be a dream, I was feeling suffocated.

I talked a lot with my husband about how I wanted to go back to work full-time, back to my previous career in project management. While he wished I would be content as a stay-at-home mom, he was supportive of me working if it was a job I could do from home. The idea of building a business of my own, not relying on a commute, a boss, or a demanding schedule, sounded most ideal and realistic with having four small kids at home.

The more conversations we had about what this could look like, the more determined I became to make this work.

My identity wasn't just "mom" anymore. I took my husband's encouragement and started researching and looking into online and remote jobs. While it felt like a step back from what I thought I wanted, I entertained the idea anyway. In this pursuit, I was praying and calling out to God. I was talking with my friends, seeking advice and suggestions. And if I'm being honest, I was not hopeful.

But God was faithful.

While in the shower one morning, God showed me the concept that is today's Genius Mom Hacks. One morning, I had a memory. Years ago, when I started getting my home on autopilot, I would write down everything I was doing. What started as a list for my own reflection and progress quickly turned into a novel of its own: pages and pages of tips, hacks, and ideas.

I dredged up the Word doc on my computer, started reading what I wrote down all those years ago, and immediately thought, *This would be so helpful for moms.* It was in the shower that one morning, contemplating my next steps in my identity, that God reminded me and revealed to me this new business idea: Genius Mom Hacks. I got so excited.

I ran and told my husband my idea. He loved it, and it was the excitement I needed to move forward.

I got my spark back. I told my husband I didn't care if Genius Mom Hacks never made a penny. I felt called to this business, helping moms.

It gave me the identity I was looking for, and I was finally fulfilled again for the first time in a long time. Immediately, I felt a difference in myself and how I carried myself and talked about myself. It helped our marriage, and I enjoyed motherhood again.

I started waking up at 5 a.m. to get a jumpstart and work on my business for a couple of hours before kids and mom life started. I found myself constantly talking about my ideas, dreams, and hopes for Genius Mom Hacks. I started sharing routines that worked, productivity tools that helped you get more done in less time, independent play ideas to get hours of kid-free time, and good ol' tried-and-true mom hacks.

I couldn't keep it to myself. I had lived through the tears and chaos of feeling stressed by my home. I had walked through the days of drowning in decision fatigue, overstimulation, and the never-ending to-do list and mental load.

I knew too many other moms who were exactly where I used to be, so I started sharing. At first, it was a simple blog post, a routine that made bedtime easier, a hack that made dinner prep faster, or a checklist that helped you have a smoother week.

This is what I'd been needing. That's when I realized this wasn't just about hacks; it was about transformation. As I was helping other moms get their homes on autopilot, I was slowly healing myself and moving into the true me: a mom with passion, a mission, conviction, and a story to tell.

Within the first year, I wrote hundreds of pages of content, 100-plus blog posts, four guides, and grew my Instagram account to almost 100,000 followers. Genius Mom Hacks became a movement of moms eliminating their stress, reclaiming their peace, as we change the narrative of motherhood.

This journey has been nothing short of amazing. It reminded me I was still capable of building something meaningful. It showed me that my voice mattered. And that I'm making a difference.

Let's change motherhood together.

If you are struggling with this thought, you are not a bad mom. You're not an ungrateful mom because you want more. Building Genius Mom Hacks fueled me and made me an even better mom. More present, more grateful, no longer feeling resentful or empty. I had a purpose different from what motherhood provided.

My kids don't need a mom who's always available but not her

true self. They need a mom who shows them what passion looks like, who models boundaries and joy, who teaches them through her example that being a parent doesn't mean losing yourself; it means becoming more of who you're meant to be. Having something that's yours isn't selfish; it's strategic, because when you're thriving, your whole family rises with you.

It will feel hard because change is hard. You have to be willing to push through and stand your ground, even if not everyone is receptive at the beginning.

Trust your intuition and watch as everyone eventually gets on board, too. You are changing, growing, and becoming a new version of yourself.

But for me, God gave me a very clear vision. And so there wasn't going to be any pushback that was going to change my direction and my belief.

And I feel like God has blessed me a millionfold in being obedient to something that I feel He has given me. And so when there's resistance, I lean into what I feel is my calling.

If you want something bad enough, you find a way to make it happen. In the beginning, I had to wake up at 5 a.m. so I could spend a couple of hours before the kids were awake to put effort into my business, then take care of four kids all day, and work again in the evening. But it energizes you. I was feeling a little apathetic about being a mom before starting my business, and immediately, I had excitement and energy again. I finally had the motivation and excitement to wake up every day.

And I became more excited to not only do my role as a mom but also work and grow Genius Mom Hacks. And I think that's what happens when you're excited about something.

I prayed for an identity outside of motherhood, to have something that was mine, where I could use my gifts and my talents and earn an income. Not only did God answer that prayer, but He answered bigger than any of my dreams.

I think that's just a testament to God's love for us. He hears your prayers, and He wants to answer them. And He's going to answer them in bigger and better ways than you ever thought possible. We think so little of what we're capable of doing. I never would have thought I would have the brand and business that I have today, with the following: writing a book and helping tens of thousands of moms. I was simply writing blog posts and looking for an identity outside of motherhood.

Your identity is worth fighting for. You can be a mom and want something else. And I will be here cheering you on the whole way.

CHAPTER 9
THE BIGGER PICTURE: FROM WINGING IT TO WALKING IN WISDOM

I used to say all the time that I was in the thick of it, but what I have come to realize is I was winging motherhood: reacting to every snack request, laundry pile, meltdown, and calendar reminder like a fire I had to put out. I wasn't steering the ship—I was hanging off the back of it, hoping I wouldn't fall overboard.

And let's be honest, the kids could feel it. Mornings were chaotic, bedtimes were frazzled, and in between, a million micro-decisions were made with no room for error. I wasn't modeling calm; I was modeling survival.

Then I stopped winging it and started creating a home on autopilot. Creating a home on autopilot didn't just change my schedule; it changed the tone of our home. And once you get a taste of this kind of motherhood, you will never go back.

WHAT A MANAGEABLE, EASY-TO-CLEAN HOME MAKES POSSIBLE

When our home was in constant chaos, everything felt harder. Transitions with the kids were harder. I was more irritable, distracted, impatient, and running on fumes. There wasn't enough space for patience, let alone presence.

But something started to shift when I started intentionally eliminating the chaos. Not just decluttering, but building effective routines, using productivity tools, mom hacks, and independent play. Slowly, the tension in our home started to ease. Our mornings stopped feeling like a fire drill, dinner wasn't a battleground, and evenings became a time to connect, not collapse.

And the most beautiful part? My kids felt it too. They became more cooperative, more like team players, not because I forced it, but because the environment finally allowed it. Turns out, kids thrive in predictability.

Saturday afternoons, after a day of sport, we weren't dealing with a marathon cleaning session. Instead, we were able to rest and play. And for me, with fewer fires to put out, I started enjoying motherhood again. Instead of hating being home, it became my sanctuary, a place I love to be.

And now, when I help other moms eliminate their stress and get their homes on autopilot, I always tell them this: You're not just creating an easy-to-clean home. That's great and all, but now you'll be able to be a more present and patient mom, and that's the real result I'm after.

Because when the home gets lighter, everything gets easier. When you are less stressed about your home, you have more capacity and energy to handle things you can't control with your kids.

Kids are naturally going to throw curveballs and be challenging. But if your cup is already full and you're already so stressed all the time, you don't have the capacity within yourself and your own emotions to be able to handle the ever-changing challenges and battles that kids give us daily. These changes matter.

One day, my kids will tell the story of their childhood. I don't get to choose every chapter, but I do get to shape the setting. When they look back, I don't want them to remember a mom who was constantly overwhelmed, always sighing, always too busy to play, too tired to talk, or too stressed to enjoy them.

I want them to remember a mom who was present, who made it a priority to spend quality time with them and made it a priority to hear their stories and connect with them. A mom who valued connection, who was at every big moment. Not because life was always easy, but because routines made the hard things feel lighter.

That's why I built the systems. That's why I create the routines. Because when you're stuck in survival mode, it's hard to connect.

When your day is ruled by reaction and constantly putting out fires, you don't get to enjoy the good stuff. But when your home runs on rhythms instead of stress, suddenly, connection becomes possible.

And here's the part that gives me the chills: the habits I'm modeling now are shaping how they'll run their own homes one day. The way I respond to mess, chaos, or change is the tone I set. Every family reset is a model of how to work as a team. One day, they will look back and realize I provided them with the needed tools to be successful in their own homes.

And that's why I do what I do: I'm not just building a home; I'm building a place they'll want to return to.

Just recently, my kids built a huge fort that took up the entire family room. They used all the pillows, every couch cushion, every blanket; they even pulled comforters from their bedrooms and dragged in all the chairs from the dining room. Then, all four of them grabbed their Nerf guns, figured out exactly when I was going to open the door, and launched a full-on Nerf ambush. It turned into an epic Nerf gun battle and also a huge mess. But it was definitely one of those core childhood memory moments.

The past, stressed-out version of me, before I got my home running on autopilot, would have been overwhelmed by the entire scene. It would have felt overstimulating, chaotic, and messy. I would have looked at the massive fort in the middle of the room and thought, *Oh my gosh, now I have to clean all this up*. I would have focused more on the mess than the memories they were making.

But now? I know we have an easy-to-clean home. I know that teamwork is light work. I know we've built a functional, strategic home that supports moments like this. So I was able to join their fun. I stepped into their creativity, into the imaginary world they had built with that fort. And it was so much fun!

When it was time to clean up, they were all in willingly. They used their reset tools, and within minutes, the family room was back to normal, with no effort from me.

As a busy mom, I had the capacity to join in, to be present, to create those memories without feeling rushed. I didn't have to say, "Not now." I didn't have to say, "I'm busy." I didn't have to get angry or frustrated about the mess.

There was laughter. There was joy. Yes, there were messes. But more importantly, there were memories.

Creating an easy-to-clean home hasn't just saved me time, it's given me the capacity to be more present, especially with the more challenging kids. With four kids, we've seen a lot. It can get loud and chaotic, which is why I love independent play. It's such a powerful tool for regulating everyone's nervous system.

And here's the thing: loudness isn't always chaos. Often, it's laughter, creativity, and excitement. But I've found that these tools of routines, structure, and independent play create more peace and less chaos. And children thrive in structure, especially neurodivergent kids. The more structure your home provides, the calmer and safer their bodies feel.

We're very aware of this in our home, because we do have a child who gets overstimulated easily. That's why we lean heavily on independent play, structure, and consistent routines.

As our kids have gotten older, these tools have become a lifeline. They help our children stay regulated, they help us stay sane, and they keep our family life flowing smoothly.

These tools have given me hours back in my week. We all only get twenty-four hours in a day. But when you use tools that simplify your life and help things get done faster, you actually create more available time.

And the most beautiful part of that? You have more time to be a present, involved parent. Because at the end of the day, I believe that's what so many moms truly want. They just feel like there's not enough time to get there. They feel like their children are getting older by the second, and they're missing out on these moments, and they live in guilt over it. An hour or two or three hours back in your week can have huge changes in the dynamic of your home. Your children feel it.

CONCLUSION

NOW IT'S YOUR TURN

If there's one thing I want you to take away from this book, it's this:
You don't need a huge overhaul of your life and home to see the transformation. Effective routines, easy micro habits, and small daily changes add up to huge results. Motherhood doesn't have to feel like a 24/7 marathon. You get to decide.

Will you leverage the tools outlined in this book (routines, laundry hacks, *race the clock*, setting your home up to be functional, team players, and independent play) to make it feel easier, or stay stuck in the martyrdom of stress and chaos? You get to build a home that works for you, not one that constantly works against you. For a long time, I didn't believe that was possible.

As I showed throughout this book, you don't have to stay in the overwhelming rat race. I replaced frustration with systems, I swapped out survival for strategy, and slowly but beautifully, my home began to run on autopilot.

CONCLUSION

No, not a robot house where everything is perfect, but a home where routines carried us. Where kids knew what to expect. Where I wasn't the bottleneck for every single task. Where peace wasn't a once-in-a-while miracle, it was the norm.

Putting my home on autopilot didn't mean checking out. It meant my kids got the best of me, not the worst of me.

This book isn't just a collection of hacks; it's a lens into the life of another mom who's just like you. A place where your home doesn't drain you; it supports you.

Take what serves you from this book, tweak what doesn't, and make it yours because these aren't copy-and-paste tools. It's about finding what works for you—your home, your rules.

Let's build one you want to wake up to every morning. Before you close this book, I want to say something from the deepest part of my heart:

Thank you. Thank you for showing up. Thank you for being open to new ideas, new habits, and a new way of doing motherhood.

Thank you for letting me into your world, for inviting my story to speak into your story. It's not lost on me that time is your most precious resource. So the fact that you chose to spend some of it here with me in these pages means more than I can say.

When I was in the thick of my hardest season, crying on the family room floor, hating being a mom, questioning my identity and future, I couldn't have imagined that one day those same struggles would be used as a roadmap for other moms. But here we are. And if this book gave you even one deep breath, one mindset shift, one aha moment that made your home feel lighter, then every tear, every late night, every early morning, every draft of these words was so worth it. You are the reason I do this. You're not just a reader; you're the heartbeat of your home, a cycle breaker, a woman who's choosing a new way over burnout.

CONCLUSION

And I'm cheering you on every step of the way. This is only the beginning. My hope for you as you close this book is that you feel less alone. I hope you see that there's nothing wrong with you. You're simply carrying too much without the right tools.

And now you're not winging it anymore. You're walking forward with the right tools. I hope you truly believe that you can eliminate the stress caused by your home.

It's possible to create an easy-to-clean home on autopilot, and it's possible for your home to feel like your sanctuary, a place you crave to be. For your routines to feel light, and for you to love motherhood again. Because if I can do this with my mess and four crazy kids, you can too. I didn't write this book to give you another checklist to chase or another unachievable goal. I wrote it so that you can release the guilt, reclaim your peace, and start leading your home with confidence with tools that work and that more moms need to know about. Yes, the systems matter. Yes, these routines help.

But more than anything, I want you to carry this truth: You don't have to be perfect to create something beautiful. Progress over perfection wins every time.

That's the heartbeat behind everything I've shared, and that's the legacy I believe you're already beginning to create. Let's change the narrative of motherhood together. What's possible now?

If you're feeling even 1 percent lighter after reading this book, I want you to know that's huge. That's the beginning of something big, because when even one system clicks into place, everything starts to shift. You stop living in constant reaction mode, the domino effect starts to kick in, and suddenly things feel easier. You have more patience, you're more present.

I'm so excited, not just about all of the great game-changing tools I've shared, but about what they unlock for you, because you're creating a home where your kids learn teamwork, indepen-

CONCLUSION

dence, and belonging. You're modeling leadership, resilience, and grace, and you're carving out time for yourself. This isn't about doing everything at once, because remember: small changes, when made consistently over time, have huge results (as Robin Sharma points out).

One smoother bedtime, one simplified routine, one moment where you choose peace over panic, those choices start to compound. They create a home that you look back on and are so thankful you didn't give up. It all starts with one small change, with intention. Let's build it.

Reading this book is a huge step, and I hope you feel proud of yourself for taking it. But here's something I know from experience: once the last page is turned, life keeps going. That's why I've built more than just this book. I've created a whole suite of ways to support you long after the spark of inspiration.

Because as moms, we need:

- Ongoing support.
- A place to ask real-life questions.
- Accountability to stay consistent.
- And most of all, we need to know we're not doing this alone.

That's exactly why I built a collection of tools, coaching, and community designed to meet you wherever you are:

- **Digital Guides**: that provide step-by-step practical solutions for everyday challenges. A deeper dive into the tools learned in this book.
- **1:1 Coaching with Me**: personalized sessions where we create custom strategies for your home and your season of life.

CONCLUSION

- **The Genius Mom Hacks Community**:
  - Monthly group coaching calls and real-time Q&A with me.
  - Weekly challenges with plug-and-play routines and tools.
  - Behind-the-scenes videos showing exactly how to run your home on autopilot.
  - A private chat where you can ask questions, share wins, and feel supported.
  - Real mom stories that remind you—you're not behind, and you're not alone.

This isn't about giving you more to do. It's about giving you the **resources, connection, and coaching** you need to build a home that feels lighter, more livable, and full of peace.

So if this book lit a spark in you, let's keep going together. Whether you want personal coaching, bite-sized guides, or a community of moms walking the same path, you have a place here.

Because your peace matters.

Your time matters.

And most of all, *you* matter.

ACKNOWLEDGMENTS

Writing this book has been one of the most rewarding—and at times challenging—journeys of my life. I could not have done it without the love, encouragement, and support of so many people.

To my amazing husband, Mike—thank you for believing in me when I doubted myself and for holding down the fort more times than I can count so I could write. Your steady support made these pages possible.

To my four incredible children, Aiden, Ethan, Madelyn & Ryan—you are the reason behind every routine, every hack, and every word of this book. You've taught me patience, resilience, and the beauty of teamwork. Without you, there would be no Genius Mom Hacks.

To my extended family and friends—thank you for being my biggest cheerleaders and reminding me to keep going when the process felt overwhelming.

To my online community—the thousands of moms who have shared your stories, struggles, testimonies, and successes with me— you are the heartbeat of this book. Your encouragement inspired me to keep creating tools that make mom life lighter, simpler, and more joyful.

To the friends and mentors who guided me along the way—I am deeply grateful for your encouragement, steady support, and the accountability that pushed me to pursue my goals.

And finally, to every mom reading this—thank you for trusting me to be part of your journey. This book is for you.

ABOUT AMY MOTRONI

Amy Motroni is a certified life coach, content creator, and mom of four (including twins!) who knows firsthand the chaos, exhaustion, and overwhelm that come with running a busy household. Determined to trade stress for peace, she developed simple systems, daily routines, and practical tools that transformed her home—and her life.

Through her brand, Genius Mom Hacks, Amy has built a thriving online community of hundreds of thousands of moms who are ready to reclaim their time, energy, and sanity. Her guides, coaching, and resources equip moms with step-by-step strategies that actually work in real life—because she's living them, too.

When she's not coaching or creating, Amy can be found walking her neighborhood with her weighted vest, cheering from the sidelines at her kids' sports games, or enjoying lake days with her family. She is passionate about helping every mom discover that with the right tools, motherhood can feel lighter, calmer, and even fun.

Amy has been married to her husband, Mike, for fourteen years. They live in Northern California with their four amazing children.

She doesn't just teach these strategies; she lives them.

THANK YOU FOR READING MY BOOK!

Loved this book? Scan here for what's next!
Your next step toward a lighter, more peaceful home is just one scan away. Check out my additional resources, coaching, and community here.

To Download Now, Visit:

I appreciate your interest in my book and value your feedback, as it helps me improve future versions.
I would appreciate it if you could leave your invaluable review on Amazon.com with your feedback.
Thank you!